RUBEN YGUA

The Russian campaign

Contact with the author: ruben.ygua@gmail.con

The content of this work, including the spell check, is the sole responsibility of the author

Dedicated to my family

ruben ygua

1812- 1813

1812

JANUARY

1- Germany: the philosopher Jakob Friedrich Fries publishes his System der Logik. The Civil Code is enacted in the Illyrian Provinces.

2- Siege of Valencia: the French have already dug three lines of trenches, in front of the bastion of Monte Olivete, the bastion of San Vicente and another in the village of Cuarte. Mexico: by order of the viceroy, the realists of Félix María Calleja defeat Ramón López Rayón in Zitácuaro, seat of the Supreme National Governing Board of America, the city is looted and burned.

3- King Ferdinand I of the Two Sicilies was forced to approve a Constitution due to pressure from the British, on whom he depends to maintain his throne in Sicily.

4- Mexico: after several hours of fighting, José María Calleja entered Zitácuaro and the Supreme National Board of America had to move to Sultepec, although its members soon dispersed throughout Mexico, all claiming the leadership, which in practice ceased to exist.

5- Siege of Valencia: Blake orders his troops to lock themselves inside Valencia during the early morning hours; the positions that they abandon are occupied by the invaders. Suchet ordered to bomb the square that afternoon, causing great damage immediately, because the Valencians had not made preparations.

6- Valencia, Spain: Marshal Suchet urges citizens to surrender, a proposal that Blake rejects.

7- South America: the actions of Captain José Gervasio Artigas did not respect the treaty signed between Montevideo and Buenos Aires. The governor of Montevideo, Gaspar de Vigodet, sent a representative to Buenos Aires to complain and the response of the triumvirate was to give him two hours to leave the city. When informed of the incident, Vigodet declared the Treaty broken.

8 - Spain: the second and last siege of Ciudad Rodrigo begins: Arthur Wellesley, Viscount of Wellington, commanding 10,700 Anglo-Portuguese soldiers, begins the assault on the fortified city of Ciudad Rodrigo, guarded by 3,700 Frenchmen under General Barrié, who have rebuilt and reinforced the fortifications remarkably after conquering it in the previous site. That same day, before the fear of the arrival of reinforcements to the place sent by Marmont, Wellington orders a risky assault of infantry. At night, the allies take the redoubt Renaud, on the hill of San Francisco.

9 - Taking of Valencia: the French advance until occupying the suburbs of Ruzafa, the bastion of San Vicente, defended by General Zayas with determination, and Cuarte; In addition, the besiegers take other strategic points, such as the convent of Santa Ursula. As the defense against an assault is unsustainable, Blake decides to capitulate. All of Blake's army is captured: 15,200 infantrymen, 1,400 horsemen, 900 officers, 400 artillerymen, 240 engineers and 23 generals; besides 22 flags and the 400 guns of the army and the square. It has been one of the worst Spanish defeats of the War of Independence. Suchet will enter Valencia the next day.

10 - France occupies Swedish Pomerania. Spain: the Cortes de Cadis founded the University of León, in Nicaragua, the last created by Spain in America, the works begin in 1816.

11- South America: Artigas signs an alliance with the Assembly of Paraguay against the Portuguese army of Diogo de Sousa, which remains in the Banda Oriental (Eastern Bank).

12- Spain: Tarifa is defended by General Francisco de Copons and Colonel Skerret, commanding the British allies, and has a total of 2,500 men as a garrison, but its walls are old and not very solid, so they dig trenches in the streets and open loopholes in the walls of the houses. The troops of the regiments of Ireland and Cantabria reject the assault with closed discharges of rifle, the French having to retire. After an armistice that the Spaniards granted to collect their dead and wounded, it began to rain, leaving the French trenches drowned and all their heavy artillery sunk. Today General Laval chooses to retire, after having suffered 2,000 casualties, leaving behind the pieces that he has not been able to remove from the mud and its ammunition.

13- Ciudad Rodrigo: the allies launch another assault, taking the fortified convent of Santa Cruz, and that of San Francisco already at dawn the next day. Wellington orders to start digging three trenches parallel to the fortifications of the city and to place as many batteries, each of 11 pieces of artillery. South America: Goyeneche sends Francisco Picoaga with 1,600 men to arrest a cavalry regiment and an infantry battalion of the Argentine Army, led by Major General Eustoquio Díaz Vélez to support the rebels in Cochabamba, defeat in the combat of Nazareno, near Potosí; Bolivia, the survivors return to Buenos Aires.

14- Allied artillery begins to bomb Ciudad Rodrigo with the first battery; the cannonade will be maintained for five days, during which the city will resist.

15- North America: Responding to a request for more troops to confront the barbarian Indians, Governor José Manrique writes to the mayors of New Mexico reminding them that it is strictly forbidden to own Indian slaves, buy them and sell them.

16- Mexico: the ship "Miño" enters Veracruz from La Coruña and disembarks 600 soldiers of the Asturias Infantry Regiment. Shortly after, he began the return with 4.5 million pesos that he takes to Havana.

17- Mexico: Rosendo Porlier and Asteguieta attack the insurgents in the ravines of Tecualoya; a battle begins that will last three days.

18- Mexico: the ship "Algeciras" arrives in Veracruz with 600 soldiers of the Lobera Regiment destined to reinforce the royalist forces.

19- In Ciudad Rodrigo: the second battery of the allies opens fire producing two breaches in the walls; until then the cannonade was ineffective against them. At nightfall, the allies begin the assault, ordered in columns: 3 under the command of General Picton, who attack the larger gap, another, commanded by General Crawford, attacks the slightest opening, and the rest makes a maneuver of distraction. After half an hour of combat, the allies take over Ciudad Rodrigo. It is a tough victory for the allies, who suffer 1,300 casualties, of which 689 soldiers, 68 officers and two generals died: Makinson and the veteran Crawford. The French had 2,000 deaths; the other 1,700 soldiers surrendered. Mexico: during the battle of Tecualoya General José María Oviedo, defender of the plaza, dies, shortly after General Hermenegildo Galeana arrives with 3,200 men, but these reinforcements will be insufficient, because they lose their artillery during a realistic assault.

20- Napoleon occupies Swedish Pomerania to better enforce the continental blockade. Mexico: after several days of fighting, the insurgents, under the orders of General Hermenegildo Galeana, are defeated in Tecualoya.

22-Mexico: José María Morelos manages to defeat in Tenancingo the royalist army that had beaten Galeana two days ago and recovered several pieces of artillery that he had lost.

24 - Spain: Altafulla combat.

25- The Spanish Cortes thanked the Vicomte de Wellington for the recon quest of Ciudad Rodrigo by granting him the title of Marquis of Ciudad Rodrigo.

27-South America: the members of the smallpox expedition must leave Chile and head for El Callao, in Peru.

29- Mexico: the ship "Asia" enters Veracruz, escorting from Cadiz to 5 transports, the frigates "Our Lady of the Choir", "Vicenta" and "Magdalena" and the ships "Isis" and "Fraternity" that bring troops from the Regiment of Expeditionary Infantry of America.

31- Mexico: Morelos enters the city of Cuautla, where he shoots fifty king's soldiers.

FEBRUARY -1812

1 – Spain: combat of Las Poblaciones.

2 – Spain: capitulation of Peñíscola.

6- Spain: combat of Rebollar de Sigüenza: the detachment of El Empecinado, famous guerrilla leader, is surprised by the troops of the French general Guy due to the denunciation of El Manco, lieutenant of the previous one. Hispanics lose 1,200 men this day, but the guerrilla leader manages to escape. The traitor will come to recruit a gang against El Empecinado; but most of its members will desert to join him, more famous than any other commander of the Spanish regular army: the population admires him.

7 – United States: since the end of the previous year, the territory of Louisiana has been suffering a series of earthquakes of great intensity. The most powerful occurred this day and destroyed the city of New Madrid, next to the Mississippi River. The earthquake broke the course of the river and formed waterfalls, as well as a lake that was named Reelfoot Lake. The tremors could be noticed even in points as far away as the city of New York.

9- Mexico: the royal general Calleja besieges Morelos in Cuautla.

10- France: Nicolas Appert invents the box for food storage.

11- Austria: Beethoven's fifth piano concert opens in Vienna.

12- South America: in Chile, Juan Martinez de Rozas had become strong in Concepción and did not recognize the dictatorship of José Miguel Carrera, but, through Bernardo O'Higgins, an agreement was reached through which Carrera recognized the Assembly of Government of Concepción.

13- South America: "La Aurora de Chile" appears, the first Chilean newspaper printed in the first printing house in the country, imported from the United States by order of President Carrera.

15- England: the doctor James Parkinson examined the corpse of a patient who had died with severe abdominal pain and identified the cause of his death as the perforation of the appendix, that is, he diagnosed appendicitis for the first time.

16- South America: the Constituent Congress meeting since December 1811 promulgates the first Constitution of the State of Quito.

17- London: the British Parliament was discussing a law to make the destruction of industrial machinery a capital crime. Among the few who showed sympathy for Luddism was a twenty-four-year-old young baron named George Gordon Byron, better known as Lord Byron, who delivered a famous speech against the bill in the House of Lords; however, the law was approved and 12,000 soldiers were assigned to the areas where the Luddites acted.

18- Mexico: Félix María Calleja launches a first assault against Cuautla, which was frustrated by the fortifications erected by the insurgents.

19- Mexico: After being rejected a second attack against Cuautla, Calleja decides to maintain the siege of the city with his troops, with the intention of overcoming it by hunger.

20- Central America: after managing in Cuba aid for the conquest of Cartagena, Benito Pérez Brito arrives in Portobelo, Panama, establishes the Audience of Bogotá in Panama and officially occupies the position of Viceroy of New Granada, maintaining the headquarters in Portobelo. He also exercises direct command over Panama.

21- South America: a fire destroys three blocks with valuable buildings in Guayaquil, Ecuador.

22- South America: an indigenous rebellion breaks out in Huánuco, Peru, which defeats the viceroy's troops at the battle of Ambo.

23- Mexico: victory of the insurgents of General Mariano Matamoros against the royal forces of Brigadier Ciriaco del Llano, in Izúcar, Puebla.

24 – France: a treaty signed in Paris with Prussia, in which it grants Napoleon a corps of army and free passage through its territory.

25- South America: in the Río de la Plata, the triumvirate dismisses Pueyrredón and puts Manuel Belgrano at the head of the army of the North, which installs its headquarters in San Salvador de Jujuy.

26 – The Alliance between France and Prussia is formalized.

27 – Spain: Battle of Massanet de Cabrenys. Río de la Plata: General Belgrano raises the 1st Argentine flag, in Rosario, Santa Fe, after installing a defense with canyons along the river and succeeds Pueyrredón in front of the Northern Army.

28- In Belgium: mining disaster near Liège. South America: the Chilean government of José Miguel Carrera officially receives the first accredited diplomat, the Consul General of the United States, Joel Roberts Poinsett.

MARCH -1812

2- England: Castlereagh is appointed Minister of Foreign Affairs.

3- Secret conversations between France and Austria.

4- South America: the Montevideo fleet bombs for the third time Buenos Aires, also without previous warning, as it had happened previously, the damages caused were minimum.

9- South America: José de San Martin arrives in Buenos Aires, from London; the triumvirate recognizes him as a lieutenant colonel of the Spanish army and appoints him to instruct the army in the military techniques he has learned in Spain.

10- South America: in Peru the mayor of Tarma José Gonzalez Prada, with a strong royal contingent, conquers Ambo and Huánuco, and leaves in pursuit of the 2,000 insurgent Indians, who disperse, capturing the ringleaders, the Creole Juan José Crespo and Castillo, the curator Norberto Haro and the mayor of Huamalies José Rodriguez, who are summarily tried and executed in a garrote in the main square of Huánuco.

11- Emancipation of Jews in Prussia. France: Napoleon authorizes the usage of Measures usually, the basis of the metric system.

12- North America: following the recommendations of Nicolai Rezanov, the Russians found Fort Ross, 24 km north of Bodega Bay and relatively close to the port of San Francisco, California, so Spain and Russia share the border by only time in History (the Russians will sell the fort on January 1, 1842)

13- South America: a counterrevolutionary coup turns Valdivia (Chile) into a stronghold of the Spanish.

14 – The alliance between France and Austria is signed. South America: the first Chilean newspaper Aurora de Chile deals with political philosophy, and stands in favor of the new national government.

15- South America: Frigate Captain Juan Domingo de Montverde arrives in Venezuela from Puerto Rico, with a small troop of 230 soldiers and offers freedom to black slaves to make weapons against the Republicans; this causes the rebellion of blacks causing panic among the landowners. In front of 1,550 men and without waiting for reinforcements, Montverde will conquer Valencia, Barinas, El Tocuyo and San Carlos, but since he can't leave forces of occupation, when he leaves the patriots start a rebellion in Valencia, then Montverde returns and gets a blunt victory.

16 – Spain, the fourth and last Siege of Badajoz begins: the Viscount of Wellington continues his peninsular campaign against the French marching to besiege Badajoz, commanding 15,000 allied soldiers, after crossing the Guadiana with a bridge of barges. They carry with them 3,000 tools of shoe and assault, 80,000 sandbags and 1,200 baskets. The square is occupied by General Philippon, commanded by 5,000 Frenchmen, who had gathered food for a month and a half, but scarce ammunition. However, they have repaired the destruction of the fortifications caused during the previous sites, reinforcing them and building more defense works.

17- The Dresden Conference begins. In Badajoz: the British decide to attack the bastions of Trinidad and Santa Maria, beginning to dig trenches in front of the Picuriña redoubt.

18 – Spain: recon quest of Soria. Argentina: Luis José de Chorroarín opens the first public library in Buenos Aires.

19- Badajoz: about 1,200 French people make an exit that damages the work of entrenchment. That night a flood of the Guadiana, floods the ditches, dragging the bridge of barges. In Cadiz: the first Spanish Liberal Constitution was proclaimed, "La Pepa ", which supposes the end of absolutism of the Old Regime in Spain.

20- North America: following a plan devised and executed by General George Mathews, by order of Secretary of State of the United States James Monroe, a group of 180 Georgian volunteers who calls himself "The East Florida Patriots" crosses the Saint Mary's River (Spanish-American border) and with the help of 9 warships forces the small garrison of Amelia Island, quartered in the Port of Fernandina and the governor of the island Justo Lopez, to surrender and makes the formal delivery of the territory to the United States .

22- South America: Spain sent to Venezuela a small contingent under the command of frigate Captain Domingo de Montverde, who on this day obtained a victory over the independence because the cavalry of these went to the royal side and attacked the Venezuelan infantry.

23- Secret agreement between Russia and Sweden.

24 - South America: the royalists defeat the Venezuelan separatists in the naval battle of Sorondo, on the Orinoco River. In the United States, the Boston Gazette prints a political cartoon coining the term Gerrymander, after former Massachusetts Governor Elbridge Gerry's approval.

25 – Badajoz: the allies have managed to place 28 pieces of heavy artillery in 6 batteries, which begin to bomb at dusk, action seconded by an assault of infantry, with which the allies manage to take the Picuriña redoubt, from which the Anglo-Portuguese artillery can beat the rest of the defenses.

26- Badajoz: the allies deploy another battery, directing their bombardment against the bastions of the Trinidad, Santa María and the wall between this and San Pedro, managing to open a gap in each of the aforementioned objectives, while preparing an assault against the bastion of San Roque, but this fails when the French flood the area. South America: in Venezuela Domingo de Montverde defeats Captain Manuel Felipe Gil in Carora, and takes Barquisimeto with an army mostly composed of pards, zambos, umlauts and islanders.

27- South America: an earthquake punishes Caracas and other regions of Venezuela causing 26,000 deaths. Since it was Sunday, many people were in the churches and died buried under the destruction. Captain Montverde took advantage of the chaos caused by the earthquake to make notable progress for the royal cause.

28- The Dresden Conference ends. Peace of Bucharest: the war between Russia and Turkey ends.

29- Russia: Mikhail Mikhailovich Speranski, a Francophile reformer, was exiled to Nizhny Novgorod, accused of treason by Tsar Alexander I.

31- South America: the archbishop of Caracas, the Catalan Narciso Coll y Prat, launches a campaign of accusation against the patriots as the cause of the divine wrath that caused the earthquake on the 26th.

LORD BYRON

Lord Byron publishes this year the first two songs of the Pilgrimages of Childe Harold, a poem, largely autobiographical, which describes the journeys and reflections of a young man weary of the world. Although Byron thought he was not going to succeed, he had a great reception and became famous.

APRIL-1812

3- U.S. President James Madison enacts a 90-day embargo on trade with the United Kingdom.

4- Spain: the Gazette of Madrid today published a document signed by the current King of Spain, José I Bonaparte, announcing the new rules for the War Councils of their armies in cases of desertion. Among other provisions, article 30 establishes that "... the military or employee of the Army who passes to the enemy, without the authorization of their leaders in writing, will suffer the penalty of being passed by arms ..." Since the French invasion in 1808 and the beginning of the occupation, many Spaniards had been captured in combat and imprisoned, putting their jailers in the dilemma of either being deported to prisons in France, or enlisting in the armies of the intruder monarch. Most of the Hispanic captives are transferred to the ranks of King Joseph, because often the other alternative is the summary shooting. These troops, called "Josephines" for fighting for King José, are very disloyal, and desert to join the Spanish regular armies or the guerrilla parties as soon as they have the chance. However, for their compatriots, who fight for the cause of the exiled Fernando VII and expel the "Gabachos" from Spain, all the Josephines or Frenchified Juries are traitors; and when they are arrested, they are usually killed. Thus, Spaniards who are detained by the French have little hope of life. Sensitive to this situation, the guerrilla leader Juan Martin "El Empecinado", will dare to write to the Duke of Mahón, governor of Cuenca, to try to break the vicious circle suffered by those recruited by force; in vain.

5- Mexico: The royalists surround a contingent of insurgents in Huajuapan. The besieged lacked artillery, but they melted bells to make cannons.

6 - Conquest of Badajoz, Wellington is informed that Marshal Soult's French army is approaching, and orders the assault to begin. The night of today the allies attack the breaches of the bastions of Trinidad and Santa Maria, ordered in 2 divisions, while another force scales the bastion of San Vicente and another division march against the castle of Badajoz. The French carry out closed discharges of musketry, shrapnel fire, and detonate buried bombs in the pit, while throwing incendiary barrels and stones. Many of the attackers drown in a hidden ditch dug in the bottom of the pit; to end up retiring with many casualties. A second assault, ends before the obstacles against cavalry, a bristling beams of edges that impale many avant-garde soldiers for their tight formation, stopping the momentum of their attack, and those behind back a second time.

During the next two hours, the Anglo-Portuguese troops taking part in the assaults on the breaches of the bastions of the Trinity and of Santa Maria remain immobile due to fear, without retreating into their trenches or advancing, being massacred by the bombardment of the artillery and the shots of French rifles. In the other fronts of attack, the allies take the castle and climb the San Vicente bastion, sweeping with sabers and bayonets the parapets and contiguous bastions, catching many defenders in the back. Philippon orders his troops to leave the breaches and take refuge in the fort of San Cristobal, where at 06:00 they capitulate. The French have suffered 1,300 casualties among the dead and wounded, the rest, 3,700 are captured; Spanish traitors found among them will be shot by guerrillas. The allies have 4,100 casualties, of which some 3,500 would fall during the assaults on the breaches and another 2,000 during the subsequent bombardment.

The city of Badajoz, the most besieged during the War of Spanish Independence, also suffers its most cruel looting by the Allied soldiers, its officers can not contain them, many are drunk, shoot anyone to steal the loot, even the Viscount of Wellington is threatened.

7- Caribbean: the freedman Jose Antonio Aponte, who had revolted the black slaves in the eastern department of Cuba, is hanged and his body exhibited in a cage at the entrance to Havana.

8- Russia: the capital of Finland is moved from Turku to Helsinki, when Russia's Tsar Alexander I signs an edict moving the Government Council of the Grand Duchy of Finland.

9- Spain: combat in Arlabán, the guerrilla leader Francisco Espoz y Mina is informed that a convoy with Spanish prisoners and valuables is going to France, escorted by 2,000 French. At the command of his departure and with that of Gregorio Cruchaga, he made a quick march and ambushed him in the town of Arlabán, completely surprising the French, who thought he was in the upper Aragon. The rear of the French column flees to the castle of the village. The rest, about 600, surrender; the number of dead and wounded is unknown. The valuable booty is captured and the prisoners freed.

10- Badajoz: looted goods will be placed in a market. This episode will be harshly criticized in England, as shameful, although the Spanish Cortes will thank the Vicomte de Wellington for the conquest of Badajoz, granting him the Grand Cross of San Fernando.

11 – Spain: bloody combat in Villagarcía.

12- North America: with only 110 men under his command, Lieutenant Colonel Thomas Adam Smith occupies the ruins of Fort Moose, in Florida and camps near San Augustin, but his forces are insufficient to assault the Castillo de San Marcos, and finish expelled by the Spaniards, who finally burn the remains of Fort Moose to avoid the invasion being repeated.

14 – Spain: French military incursion in Guarda.

16- Río de la Plata: in Buenos Aires, Juan José Paso and Feliciano Chiclana, members of the triumvirate that governed the United Provinces of the Río de la Plata, had maintained serious disputes between them, and both ended up presenting their resignation, but only the Paso was accepted, which was replaced by Juan Martin de Pueyrredón, who had just arrived in Buenos Aires.

17- Rio de la Plata: General Manuel Belgrano forces the bishop of Salta Nicolas Videla del Pino to leave the city accusing him of Spanish feelings, leaving the seat vacant until 1836.

19- The tensions between France and Russia reached a breaking point when Russia demands that France abandon the conquered territories in Prussia.

20- In Calcutta, India: Beginning of the voyage of explorer William Moorcroft in the Himalayas, Tibet and Kashmir. United States: death of Vice President George Clinton.

21- South America: a group of royalists exiled in Carmen de Patagones (Argentina) and led by Colonel Faustino Ansay, seizes the town and its fort, with the support of the population.

24- South America: in Venezuela Domingo de Montverde defeats Colonel Miguel Ustáriz in Colorado de San Carlos, Carabobo.

25- South America: in view of the increasingly alarming Spanish successes, the Congress of Caracas decides to replace its president, Cristobal Mendoza, with Francisco de Miranda, with more military experience, who is granted dictatorial powers.

26- Central America: Captain General José Bustamante y Guerra sends troops to quell the rebellions in Nicaragua and these occupy Masaya and Granada, agreeing with the rebels. Bustamante refuses to accept the accords and orders them to be prosecuted (16 death sentences will be issued in 1814, which will be commuted and all the condemned released by the royal pardon of 1817).

30- United States: the territory of Orleans became the State of Louisiana, the eighteenth of the United States of America. The northernmost territory, which until then had been called the District of Louisiana, became the Territory of Missouri.

MAY-1812

1- Río de la Plata: the Portuguese, who had invaded Uruguay the previous year, return to Brazil.

2- Mexico: Morelos manages to escape from Cuautla with his men, avoiding the fence established by Calleja. He finally enters the city after a long siege started on February 9, his men make a killing among its inhabitants, for having welcomed the insurgents, Colonel Francisco Ayala, who commanded the infantry, is shot and Leonardo Bravo, who he had fortified Cuautla, was executed by garrote.

8- Río de la Plata: combat of the Rincon, in Santa Fe; Argentina, 17 royal corsairs from Montevideo who disembark to obtain meat are attacked by the Blandengues de la Frontera of Santa Fe under the command of Second Lieutenant Juan Pablo Videla; 10 drown when trying to return to their boat and the rest captured because they do not carry weapons, five will be shot immediately.

9- The French emperor Napoleon Bonaparte decides to break diplomatic relations with Russia, rejecting the proposals of the Tsar regarding the Continental Blockade imposed by France, broken by the Russian Empire at the end of last year. Bonaparte considers that Tsar Alexander has breached the agreements of Erfurt signed in 1810. This violation justifies for the French emperor any invasion of Russian territory.

11- London: when British Prime Minister Spencer Perceval was entering the House of Commons, a man approached and shot him in the chest with a gun. The murderer, who made no attempt to escape, was named John Bellingham, and was a merchant who had been unjustly imprisoned in Russia and who had made several requests to the government to collect compensation, but all had been rejected. Perceval is the only English Premier killed in history.

15- Spain: the ship "Asia" arrives in Cadiz, coming from Veracruz, transporting 7 million pesos.

16- The Emperor Napoleon Bonaparte leaves France under the command of part of his army, entering the Confederation of the Rhine, to reach Dresden at the end of the day. The Treaty of Bucharest is signed, ending the Russo-Turkish war and annexing Bessarabia to Russia, and the Ottoman Empire gave up its aspirations on Georgia.

17- Dresden, Germany: Napoleon meets the kings of Saxony, Prussia and the Emperor of Austria.

18 – Spain: Combat of the Almaraz Bridge.

21- Alexander I moves to Vilna, near the border; the tsar tries until the last moment to avoid war, as his foreign minister, Rumyantsev, declared to the French ambassador, Lauriston.

22- England: Felling mine disaster, a mine explosion at the Felling colliery near Jarrow, leaves 96 dead.

24- South America: combat of Pocona or Quehuiñal, in Bolivia, the royalists of José Manuel de Goyeneche defeat the rebels of Esteban Arce, which allows them to attack and sack Cochabamba a few days later, despite the defense of their women (the "heroines of La Coronilla").

25- South America: in order to raise the spirits of his troops, Manuel Belgrano presents a flag of his creation formed by two light blue strips separated by a white band.

26- The government of the United Provinces of the Rio de la Plata signed with Portugal the Rademaker-Herrera treaty, by virtue of which Portugal agrees to withdraw its army from the Banda Oriental. The treaty was signed by the pressure of the British, who were allies of the Spaniards and knew that Spain did not see with good eyes the Portuguese invasion, although its purpose was theoretically to fight the independence. The treaty was negotiated and signed in Buenos Aires, but Diogo de Sousa refused to comply. When it was communicated to Rio de Janeiro, the Portuguese government considered that Rademaker had exceeded its concessions and neither accepted it.

27- Mexico: José María Morelos defeats the Royalists in Escamela.

28 – Spain: combat of Tudela.

29- Napoleon resumed his march to the East, crossing Prussia, en route by Glogay, Poznan and Danzig, until arriving at Kovno, grouping along the way a Grande Armée of some 420,000 soldiers, plus his auxiliary personnel. Another 80,000 will be recruited soon in Lithuania, but will not participate in the campaign. In Prussia and Poland another 70,000 soldiers guard the borders of the French Empire, stationed between the Vistula and the Oder.

31- The murder of Perceval took place at the worst possible time, as negotiations between Britain and the United States were being finalized to put an end to the trade restrictions that Great Britain had up to now. President Madison felt that he could no longer contain the pressure of those who considered that war should be declared to Great Britain, so this morning he submitted it to deliberation in Congress. The debate was heated, because the New England States were pro-British and against, while those in the south and those in the west were pro-French and in favor. In the end the war was declared by 79 votes in favor and 49 against in the House of Representatives and by 19 to 13 in the Senate.

JUNE-1812

1- Spain: second combat of Bornos or Guadalete. Marshal Soult, commander in chief of the French army of Andalusia, decides to fortify Bornos, to improve the supply route between Seville and the troops that are besieging Cadiz, sending General Corroux there with 4,500 soldiers. When the Spaniards learned of the plan, General Ballesteros left Gibraltar at the command of a similar force, forded the Guadalete River and attacked the French, who were already billeted in the village. After an initial Spanish success, Corroux responds by trying to wrap Hispanics on his left flank. Some rookies flee in disarray when seeing the French cavalry, which motivates the disorder of all the formation of Ballesteros. The rest of the regiments flee, while others retreat in good order, protecting them; which does not prevent Hispanics from having 1,500 casualties at the end of the day.

2- Metternich, Austrian Foreign Minister, tells Tsar Alexander I that his troops will not support Napoleon in the event of a war between France and Russia.

4- North America: Infantry Brigadier Sebastian Kindelan and Oregon, governor of Eastern Florida, gathers troops of Cuban blacks and recruits Seminoles and fugitive slaves to fight the invading Georgians, offers rewards to the Seminoles for the delivery of leather scalps of Anglo-American invaders.

5- In South Africa: colonization of Zuurveld; foundation of Grahamstown Fort.

6- Italy: Duke Francisco IV of Modena marries his niece María Beatriz Victoria de Saboya, daughter of King Victor Manuel I of Sardinia and his sister María Teresa.

8- England: Robert Jenkinson is appointed Prime Minister.

10- South America: the revolutionaries of Quito enter the convent where the old former president of the Audience, Manuel de Urriés, took refuge and beat him up, dying as a result of his wounds.

11 - Spain: Battle of Maguilla, a British cavalry brigade led by Major General John Slade attacked a similar-sized French cavalry brigade commanded by General of Brigade Charles Lallemand. The British dragoons scored an initial success, routing the French dragoons and capturing a number of them. The British troopers recklessly galloped after their foes, losing all order. At length, the French reserve squadron charged into the British, followed by the French main body which rallied. With the tables turned, the French dragoons chased the British until the horses of both sides were too exhausted for the battle to continue.

12- Spain: the allies leave Fuenteguinaldo and go in three columns towards Salamanca. The allied army is made up of 30,500 Englishmen, 18,000 Portuguese from General Beresford, and 3,300 Spaniards from Carlos of Spain, including the spearmen of "El Charro", totaling some 47,800 infantrymen, 3,200 horsemen and 40 cannons.

13- South America: the Argentine brigantine "Hiena", of 15 guns and manned by 83 men, the majority British and North American, to the control of Tomas Taylor, mocks the blockade of Buenos Aires and goes to Carmen de Patagones, to try to suffocate the rebellion of colonel Faustino Ansay, but the royalists seize him and take him to Montevideo, incorporating him into the Spanish Armada.

14- London: the new British government lifted all restrictions on trade with the United States.

15 – Spain: second siege of Astorga, by Spanish troops of Santocildes. United States: New York State charters the City Bank of New York.

16- Spain: the French army of Portugal, commanded by Marshal Marmont, Duke of Ragusa, is stationed in Salamanca, with some 37,000 soldiers. When informed of the Allied advance, he left for Toro, leaving behind 800 men in the fortified convents of San Cayetano, Merced and San Vicente.

17 – Spain: Wellington besieges the forts of Salamanca: the allies barricade themselves in San Cristobal and attack the fortifications of Salamanca by shelling them with heavy artillery brought from Almeida. Those of Cayetano and La Merced are assaulted and taken by the infantry; and that of San Vicente surrenders. Marmont decides to return to Salamanca when it is already too late, and the English force him to retreat back to Toro and Tordesillas. The French, in the left margin of the Duero, receive reinforcements of the army of Asturias, happening to add the cash of the army of Portugal about 47,600 infants, 3,400 horsemen and 78 guns.

18- United States: President Madison signs the declaration of war against Britain without knowing that the casus belli had disappeared. When the news crossed the Atlantic Ocean in both directions, both countries learned that they were at war over an issue that had already been resolved. But the American warmongers were not going to let such minutia ruin them for several months of campaigning, so they got the United States to demand more conditions from Britain, it refused and the war broke out anyway.

19- In Eastern Europe: accompanying the Grand Army, the columns and convoys of supplies extend for several kilometers, traveling along parallel roads. Bonaparte had to organize a network of warehouses throughout the European route of his army, the largest in Western military history until then.

20- Pope Pius VII remained a prisoner of Napoleon, although all his attempts to wrest any kind of concession had been useless. The emperor decided to transfer him secretly from Savona to Fontainebleau to deal personally with the matter. This afternoon he arrived at his new place of captivity. I was very sick. On the way he had come to receive the extreme anointing. Napoleon was embarrassed when the Pope called him "my dear son" and added: "a son a little stubborn, but a son alike".

21- Spain: British troops of Popham enter Lekeitio.

THE GREAT ARMY THAT NAPOLEON WILL LEAD TO RUSSIA

Napoleon mobilizes some 324,000 infantry, 96,000 horsemen, 110,000 specialized soldiers, such as 20,000 sappers or the 21,000 employees in artillery or supply trains, and non-combatant military auxiliary personnel, such as health workers or cooks; 180,000 horses, and 580 guns. In total, the Grande Armée will reach some 610,000 men in campaign, counting on the Lithuanians. Some 300,000 soldiers are French: 4,000 are with Napoleon in his General Headquarters, the Imperial Guard, among all its different units, such as the Cuirassiers, Carabineers, the Young Guard and the Old Guard, totaling 47,000; the 1st Davout Corps, 72,000; the 2nd of Oudinot, 37,000; the 3rd of Ney, 40,000; the 9th of Victor, 33,000; the 10th of MacDonald, 32,000; and the 11th Reserve, Augerau, 27,000. To these infantry bodies are added the Cavalry Reserve Corps: 1st of Nansouty, with 12,000 horsemen; the 2nd Montbrun, with 10,000; 3rd of Grouchy, with 10,000; and the 4th of Latour Mobourg, with 8,000; all under Murat.

The rest come from allied or occupied countries: the 5th Corps of Poniatowsky, of 36,000 Poles, the Austrian, of Schwarzenberg, of 30,000 Austrians, the 6th of Saint Cyr, of 25,000 Bavarians; the 7th of Renier, of 17,000 Saxons, the 4th of the Eugene, with 45,000 Italians, the 8th of Vandamme, of 18,000 Westphalians; the 20,000 Prussians of MacDonald and another 12,000 Wuer- burgesses framed in several French corps. Finally we would have to mention 4 Swiss regiments, 3 Portuguese and 1 Spanish regiment, taken from the remains of the expedition to Denmark, prisoner in Mainz.

Another 80,000 men will be recruited in Lithuania, deploying near the borders of Prussia. In total, troops from some 21 countries will integrate the Grande Armée.

22- South America: royalist forces from Chiloe land in Carelmapu and conquer Osorno, in Los Lagos; Chile.

23- South America: due to the great desertion of patriotic soldiers, Francisco de Miranda arranges the incorporation of a thousand slaves to the Venezuelan army, offering them freedom if they are active for 4 years and participate in outstanding combats. Miranda will be criticized for the social destabilization that this measure may cause.

24- Napoleon, in front of the Grand Army, crosses the Niemen River invading Russia without declaration of previous war, the tsar seeks allies. Throughout the night the long columns of invading soldiers cross the Niemen River, border between Prussia and Russia. They do it for four bridges made by engineers near the towns Kovno, Olitt, Merech and Jurburg. The crossing operation will last for 3 days.

Alexander leaves Vilna to return to Moscow, without naming a commander-in-chief of his armies, who act without coordination in the face of the Napoleonic invasion. Barclay de Tolly assumes command to be minister of the Czar's war. He plans a counterattack for July 14, but the two main Russian armies are still far apart.

25- Napoleon has not sent any declaration of war to Czar Alexander I, because he hopes to subject him with an offensive to Moscow or St. Petersburg, although he hopes to defeat the Russian armies in a great confrontation before arriving at Smolensk; in principle, it does not intend to extend its supply line beyond this city.

Napoleon sends the 2nd and 10th Army Corps of Marshal Oudinot and Macdonald to cover his left flank in northwest Russia.

26- The Russian Tsar, supported by the Orthodox Church, decides to appeal to the national and religious sentiments of his subjects to encourage a massive popular mobilization, proclaiming that this will be "The Great Patriotic War of Mother Russia"

The Russian army is deploying in a strip of about 1,000 km, organized into three armies of 230,000 soldiers and 988 guns: the 1st Western Army, commanded by Barclay de Tolly, with 130,000 soldiers and 550 guns, approaching St. Petersburg; the 2nd Western Army, commanded by the Prince of Bagration, with 45,000 soldiers and 270 guns, near Moscow; and the 3rd Reserve Army, commanded by Tormasov, with 46,000 soldiers and 168 guns, maneuvering towards Kiev.

The French troops enter Polotsk and continue advancing to the east in parallel to the Grande Armée, but they encounter a strong Russian resistance in Jabukowo and Kliatstitsy, having to retreat back to Polotsk.

27- Napoleon tries to locate the bulk of the Russian army looking for a decisive battle, and order Marshal Murat, commanding two cavalry corps with 60 pieces of light artillery, to march towards Vilna and engage combat with any Russian force in the vicinity.

28 – Russia: Napoleon captures the city of Vilna, the troops of the 1st Western Army of Barclay de Tolly, about 100,000 men, have evacuated the city, burning the warehouses and the bridge behind them; they started retreating two days ago to the fortified Drissa. Bagration in turn retracts his Western Army towards Nesvizh.

29- Bonaparte stops the march, camping in Vilna, wondering why the Russians have refused to fight and where they will stop in their retreat. In the afternoon he is informed of the situation of his troops in Spain, which worsens daily.

30- Napoleon sends to the 2nd French Army Corps commanded by Marshal Oudinot, about 29,000 men and 114 cannons, supported by the 10th Corps of MacDonald, with some 32,000 soldiers, to cover the left flank of his advance, having to march north, towards Riga and St. Petersburg.

South America: the royalists imprisoned in Puerto Cabello, Venezuela, rebel, manage to control the city and capture the separatists who were in it, including Simon Bolívar.

JULY -1812

1- The Prince of Wittgenstein has 17,000 men and 108 cannons of the Finnish Army with them they must stop the French advance towards Saint Petersburg. In Vilna Napoleon receives the Russian general Balashov, who transmits a message to him of the czar Alexander, proposing peace conversations, with the previous condition that it retires the army of Russia. Napoleon rejects the offer.

2- Camped in Vilna, Napoleon is in charge of the administration of Lithuania, recruiting 80,000 inhabitants to protect his supply lines from Prussia; in addition Kobrin leaves the 7th Corps of Renier.

3- South America: Argentines shoot the former mayor of Buenos Aires Martin de Alzaga, and more than 30 people, accused of conspiring in favor of a Spanish restoration.

4- Russia: Napoleon accepts the idea of Tadeusz Matuszewicz of a confederation of the szlachta, which declares the restoration of the kingdom of Poland, to which adheres insurgent Lithuania. Mexico: José Maria Morelos defeats the royalists in Zitlala.

5- United States: the territory of Louisiana that is not part of the new State of Louisiana is baptized as the Territory of Missouri, to avoid confusion.

6- The restoration of commercial relations between Russia and England is announced. In the city of Orebro a treaty of peace and anti-French military alliance between Russia and England is signed, to which the kingdom of Prussia and the Austrian Empire will be signed with different agreements, within 6 and 7 months respectively; therefore this Sixth Coalition against France will not come true until next year.

7 – Spain: British troops commanded by Cotton enter Castro.

8 – Russia: combat of Karelichy, between Russians and Poles.

10- Russia: the Polish cavalry of Rozniecki is beaten by the Cossacks of Platov at the Battle of Mir.
North America: Comanche Indians and Tonkawa once again assault the village of San Marcos de Neve in Texas and take 205 horses. When some Comanche inform the San Antonio authorities that this is a large multi-ethnic campaign to wage war on the Spanish border, the governor Manuel Maria de Salcedo withdraws the small garrison of San Carlos and its inhabitants, fed up with floods and that the Indians prevent them from cultivating their fields, abandon it (it will be repopulated as San Marcos in its current place by Anglos in 1846). Shortly after the commander Joaquin de Arredondo will order the construction of a large fort in the same area, but the workers will abandon the project, since they will be attacked by Comanche every time they go out to look for wood or supplies.

12- North Sea: a small British fleet destroyed in Lyngor the last remnant of the Danish fleet, the frigate Najaden, which sank, leaving 133 dead and 82 wounded.

14- Russia: Tsar Alexander appears in public in St. Petersburg to harangue and try to raise the morale of the population.

15- The United States plans a triple invasion of Canada: from Lake Champlain to Montreal and Quebec, from Niagara to the west and from Detroit to the east. However, the offensive from Champlain was never carried out, because it required soldiers from New England and that State is opposed to "the war of Mr. Madison", as it is called. The invasion from Detroit is assigned to General William Hull, who began preparations this morning.

16- Napoleon resumes the offensive, leaves Vilna to the east, the French leave in the city about 3,000 soldiers sick and some injured by the poor state of the roads, is the first casualties of the Grande Armée, which will soon begin to lack supplies, because the convoys cannot follow closely the army in march. Large numbers of French horses will suffer colic, after Murat refuses to wait for the grain transport wagons.

17- Spain: during the following weeks both armies will make several marches between Toro and Tordesillas. Through this locality the French cross the Douro tonight. United States: the British are ahead of the American preparations and take the initiative, attacking and conquering Fort Mackinac, on Mackinac Island, on Lake Michigan, the Indians of the area allied with the British; Chief Tecumseh received the degree of Brigadier General.

18- Russia: Napoleon sends part of the 1st French Army Corps, some 56,000 soldiers under Marshal Davout, to Mogilev, to prevent the 2nd Western Russian Army of General Bagration from joining the 1st Western Army of Barclay de Tolly. Spain: the French arrive at the Guareña River, to the left of the Allied deployment, forcing Wellington to reorder their positions and retreat to San Cristobal

19- Spain: the French advance crossing the river Tormes between Alba and Huerta. Wellington deploys his troops in the small hill of Arapiles on his left, to Santa Marta on his right, with vanguard in Calvarrasa de Abajo and the rearguard covering the road to Ciudad Rodrigo; its headquarters is in the same town of Arapiles. Marmont locates his troops before the small Arapil, occupying Calvarrasa de Arriba, the mount of Our Lady of la Peña and the hill Arapil Grande.

20- Russia: Davout's troops enter Mogilev on the banks of the Dnieper, capturing important deposits of Russian weapons and supplies. In Spain: combats of Castrejón and Castrillo.

21- Russia: in a skirmish, 6 km from Mogilev, the vanguard of the 2nd Russian Western Army of Bagration, formed by cavalry troops commanded by Count Sievers, is attacked by a regiment of Davout French cuirassiers. The Russians surround them, causing 500 dead and wounded, capturing another 200; the rest flee. Spain: first Battle of Castalla. The Spanish General O'Donell and the Viscount of Wellington provide that a flotilla of Anglo-Spanish ships anchored before Denia and Cullera, in Valencia, as protection to the disembarkation of an Anglo-Sicilian contingent from Palermo, and as a lure to attract French troops and cover up the Spanish main attack against them. The Marshal Suchet, informed of the eventual Allied landing, sends to the area from Alcoy to 2 regiments and 2 brigades of the division of General Harispe, 4,000 men, deploying them between Ibi, Castalla, where General Delort, Onil, and Blair camp. On the morning of July 21, O'Donell places his 11,000 soldiers between Ibi and Jijona, on his right flank, passing through Castalla in its center, to Petrel, on his right. The reserve was located in Venta de Tibi, and the cavalry, in Villena. The Spaniards attack the French brigade stationed at Ibi, then troops from the center and the left of Spain attack General Delort's regiment at Castalla, at the center of the French deployment, expelling him from the town and occupying it, while the Gallic troops regroup and their cavalry coming from Onil and Blair is hidden in some olive groves. The regiment of French dragons ambushed in the olive grove assaulted the forces of O'Donell in advance, attacking Castalla near the central body by the flank of their march, making him flee in disarray, avoiding only a massacre the intervention of the reserve troops; but the French take many prisoners. The evicted French brigade of Ibi returns to counterattack the town, although the Spaniards there entrenched resist. Finally, General Harispe leaves from Alcoy regrouping the French, retreating to Alicante, after losing 800 soldiers among dead or wounded, and another 2,800 prisoners, along with 2 cannons and 3 flags. Hispanic casualties are estimated at 1,000 dead or wounded and 2,130 prisoners, inadmissible given the initial Spanish superiority. General O'Donnell will be blamed for the disaster by not waiting for the landing of the Allied division, and will also be accused of having been absent from the battlefield at the most difficult times.

22- Russia: When Davout sends 28,000 men to the town of Saltanovka, Bagration sends General Raevsky's Army Corps to expel them, with a load of bayonet infantry, seconded by his own sons, and the French withdraw. The Russians suffer 2,500 casualties and the French about 5,000. Spain: Battle of Arapiles or Salamanca. Arthur Wellesley, Viscount of Wellington, decides to resume allied offensive operations in Spain with the aim of liberating Madrid, realizing that Napoleon has taken French troops from the Iberian Peninsula, such as the Imperial Guard and the Polish Lancers, to join them to the Great Armée of his Russian campaign. At 2:00 pm, Marmont orders Generals Thomieres and Macune to advance from the Arapil Grande to their left, to flank the British on their right and cut off the escape route. At 10:00 o'clock Wellington decided to prepare the march to Ciudad Rodrigo, but he notices that the division of Thomieres is too far to the west of the division of Macune. At 15:30 hours, Wellington orders the 3rd Infantry Division and D'Urban's cavalry brigade to attack the enemy's left to surround it by the Zuguen stream. Marmont arranges that the cavalry of Curto go to defend them, being overwhelmed by the British cargo, leaving exposed to the division of Thomieres, beaten about 40 minutes later, disbanding and being pursued by the English riders. Towards 16:00 hours, Wellington orders the 4th and 5th infantry divisions and two brigades of Portuguese cavalry attack the division of Macune and the Claussel division is in the Arapil Grande, in the French center. Macune orders his troops to form in pictures and repel the assaults of the infantry, but a charge of the heavy dragons of Le Marchand breaks his lines towards 4:45 pm, forcing him to retreat. The division of Claussel stops in the Arapil Grande the attack of the 4th English division of General Cole with a heavy fire, towards 16:30 hours. Reject the English cavalry and start a counterattack towards the small Arapil, contained by the 6th division of Clinton. The French withdraw at 5:30 p.m., and the allies converge towards where the remnants of the Thomieres and Macunne units are grouped. Marmont is wounded in the arm and right flank, succeeding General Bonnet, but this is also achieved, leaving the French army of Portugal about 20 minutes without any leadership, until General Claussel takes over. By then, around 6:00 p.m., the 1st English division of Campbell assaults the Arapil Grande; the French division of General Foy who defended it is withdrawn. Harassed, with no center or left flank, Claussel orders the retreat towards 7:00 pm, retiring his army in good order, protected by what remains of his right wing. The French are persecuted by the allied cavalry until Peñaranda, the Englishmen will reproach the Spaniards for not having cut the French withdrawal on the bridge of Alba de Tormes; if he had done it, the enemy's defeat would be absolute. The French have 7,000 casualties, General Ferey being killed, with his division protecting the French retreat, Thomieres and Desgraviers, another 7,000 more are captured, seizing 20 guns and 9 flags. The allies suffered 4.700 casualties; among his dead is General Le Marchant, inventor of the fearsome sword of the English cavalry, killed at the head of a charge. For this crucial victory, one of the most important of the Napoleonic Wars, Wellesley will be decorated with the Order of the Golden Fleece by the Spanish Regency and promoted to the Marquis of Wellington by the British court. This defeat will mean for Soult the withdrawal of his French army from Andalusia. King Jose himself, who came to reinforce Marmont with 10,000 soldiers, retreated to Madrid.

23 – Russia: Bagration attacks Mogilev with a total of 60,000 Russians against the remaining 28,000 men of Davout. These, well entrenched in the stronghold, compensate for their inferiority and reject the Russians, who suffer 4,000 casualties by about 1,000 of the French. Spain: Combat of Garcia Hernandez. General Bock, with only four cavalry squadrons, some 450 horsemen, attacks three French battalions commanded by General Foy, who retreat from the battlefield of Arapiles. These form in frame, but it is broken by the impetuous German charge; being many stabbed. The Germans suffer 150 casualties, for 1,400 of the French; one of the most disproportionate cavalry actions in history. Mexico: José María Morelos arrives in

Huajuapan and puts to flight the royalists who besieged her, abandoning all her artillery and many horses.

24- Spain: King Joseph Bonaparte, who came to help Marmont in Arapiles through the port of Guadarrama, returns quickly to Madrid, after being informed of the rapid Allied advance.

25- Russia: Bagration refolds all its 2nd Army, crossing the Dnieper. The Russians will not be able to assemble their armies until after ten days, in Smolensk. South America: in Venezuela the royalist Domingo de Montverde advances unstoppable to Caracas, Miranda is forced to negotiate the surrender of the rebels, which was signed in San Mateo this afternoon. Insurgents agree to lay down their arms in exchange for immunity for their people and your assets.

26 – Russia: combat of Ostrowno and Battle of Kobrin: Russian general Konovnitsyn is attacked at 08:00 hours from two flanks by the French infantry commanded by Eugene and Murat's cavalry. The Russians repel three cavalry attacks, ending up annihilating a Croatian battalion; the French disbanded until the intervention of Murat himself; another attack dislodges the Russians from their positions, around 3:00 p.m. Napoleon arrives on the battlefield and cancels Eugene's order to cease the offensive. The soldiers of Konovnitsyn retreat in good order along the road to Ostrowno, offering strong opposition to the French, but losing hundreds of men. They arrive in the afternoon to Komarovo, where they receive more Russian reinforcements from Barlcay de Tolly. At night, this contingent camps in Vitebsk and is integrated into the 3rd Corps under the command of Tuchckov, whose mission is to protect the retreat of the 1st Western Army of Barclay by cutting the road to Ostrowno. Bonaparte decides to delay his attack on the Russian 1st Army to hope to gather more men. On the same day, General Tormasov, of the 3rd Russian Army, makes a counterattack aimed at Brest and Kobrin, where this great part of the 3rd Corps of Reiner, and Yanov. The attack eliminates three squadrons of Austrian horsemen; at dusk the Russians evict the Saxon Hussars and Ulaans from Brest and take 40 prisoners.

27- Russia: the troops of the 3rd Russian Army attack Kobrin, defended by a detachment of the 3rd Corps under Klenchel who has fortified the square and placed cannons on it. Their rifles and artillery stop a Russian assault, but a second charge of cavalry makes them retreat to the suburbs, where they move a battery and barricade themselves again in a monastery, covering the only access bridge. Finally, the Russians make several consecutive charges of cavalry and infantry to the bayonet, taking the bridge and the monastery, until they take the last fortified building. The rest of the defenders of Klenchel surrenders: the French lose 3,000 men among dead, wounded and prisoners, the first defeat in their Russian campaign. Napoleon awaits the troops he needs to attack Vitebsk the next day, July 28. But Barclay has had time to retreat east and avoid the fight.

28- Russia: The Prince of Wittgenstein concentrates his troops near Kliastitsy, while Oudinot sends a reconnaissance division under Legrand to Yakubovo.

29- Russia: Combats of Yakubovo and Kliastitsy: Russian vanguard, commanded by General Kulnev, attacks the French with superior forces; the division of Verdier comes to the aid of Legrand, while two regiments of Cuirassiers and an artillery company reinforce the Russians. South America: being informed that a Peruvian army of 3,000 soldiers under General Pio Tristan is advancing towards Jujuy, Manuel Belgrano, following orders from Buenos Aires, urged the population to evacuate the city in the direction of Córdoba without leaving anything that could be useful to the enemy. Harvests and houses had to be burned. Taking into account that he threatened to shoot anyone who did not comply with the order, nobody put up resistance and the exodus from Jujuy was carried out as planned.

30- Russia: the Russians resume their offensive, Oudinot mobilizes the rest of his corps to envelop the Russian left while fighting back its center, but the soldiers of Kulnev reject attacks with heavy artillery fire; then the Russians initiate a counterattack pushing the French in the direction of Kliastitsy, from where they are expelled by the assault on the bayonet of the Grenadiers of the Pavlovsky regiment. The French are persecuted by the Hussars of Grodno regiment. Spain: Wellington enters Valladolid.

31- South America: Miranda is captured by Montverde when he tried to embark on La Guairá. Further south, this same day a royalist corsair captures a schooner and two Paraguayan merchants at the confluence of the Paraná and Santa Fe rivers.

AUGUST -1812

1- Russia: the hussars of Grodno are scattered by a French counterattack in Boyarsina. Kulnev is killed by a cannon shot in action. Oudinot will try to take Kliastitsy, but will be rejected by Wittgenstein in the Drissa, retiring to Polotsk. Spain: Wellington captures the city of Cuellar.

2- Russia: take of Polotsk, the 60,000 French soldiers of Oudinot and MacDonald will stay in the city and no longer participate in the main campaign, making it an important enclave to protect the rear of the Bonaparte expedition and its supply route; This will shortly send the 6th Corps of Saint Cyr, some 13,000 Bavarians, to reinforce this garrison, and later the 9th Corps of Victor, with more than 30,000 French. These troops will remain in the Polotsk region until October.

3 - Russia: Combat of Gorodeczna, Bonaparte, with 175,000 soldiers, pursues the 130,000 Russians of the 2nd Western Tsar Army, commanded by Bagration, which eludes a large-scale confrontation, preferring to contain the invaders in limited struggles, retreating into the interior of Russia .Bagration arrives this day at Smolensk, joining forces with the 1st Army of Barclay de Tolly.

4- South America: José de San Martin founded a Masonic lodge in Buenos Aires, which he named Lodge Lautaro, in honor of the Araucanian chief who led the resistance against the Spaniards in the 16th century. The Lautaro Lodge was soon associated with the Patriotic Society of the Morenoites, beginning to oppose the government of the triumvirate. United States: when General Hull learned that Mackinac Island had fallen into British hands and that they had received the support of Indian tribes, he aborted Canada's invasion plans and prepared to march against the British.

5- South America: in Venezuela Francisco de Miranda was preparing to embark for Great Britain when he was captured in the port of La Guairá by a group of officers (among whom was Simon Bolivar) who considered their capitulation to the Spaniards a betrayal. They accused him of embezzling public funds and handed him over to the Spanish authorities, who imprisoned him in Puerto Cabello. Bolivar, "as a reward for the service rendered to the King of Spain with the delivery of Miranda", received a safe conduct to go into exile abroad.

6- Spain: the vanguard of Wellington pursues the withdrawal of King Joseph's troops through Segovia and the ports of Guadarrama and Navacerrada to Madrid.

7- United States: Tecumseh, commanding two dozen Indian warriors, attacks about two hundred American militants near Brownstown, who, in panic, were put to flight, there were 18 dead, 12 wounded and 70 missing.

8 - Russia: combat of Inkowo; Platov's Cossacks capture 300 French.

9- United States: 75 British soldiers, 60 Canadian militiamen and 70 Indians under the command of Tecumseh attacked some 600 US soldiers (half of them militiamen) in Maguaga.

The combat was a succession of errors: the British confused their Indian allies with enemies and a horn bug was mistakenly interpreted as a withdrawal order. The Americans did not take advantage of the British confusion, cowering they remained hidden even after the British had retired.

10- Mexico: the insurgents had been besieged at the beginning of April in Huajuapan, Oaxaca by General Jose Maria de Regules Villasante, but Jose Maria Morelos manages to free them, causing the Royalists 400 dead and the loss of 30 cannons, with which Morelos reinforces its 2,500 men and enters Tehuacan de las Granadas.

11 – Spain: combat of Majadahonda. King Joseph Bonaparte is forced for the second time to leave Madrid leaving a garrison of 2,500 men in El Retiro to hinder the Allied persecution. At 10:00 today, the allies enter the capital through the door of San Vicente, arriving in first place the guerrillas Juan Martin, "El Empecinado" and Don Juan Palarea, "The Doctor", together with the Viscount of Wellington, cheered with great joy by the euphoric population.

12 – Russia: combat of Rassasna. Spain: Arthur Wellesley in Madrid: after the battle of Arapiles, the road to Madrid of the allies of the Viscount of Wellington is open, and the communication lines between the French troops stationed in the north and the Spanish southwest are threatened, for which reason Soult decides to evacuate his forces from Andalusia and retreat to the northeast; Castile and Leon will also be unguarded. Mexico: General Nicolas Bravo defeats the royalist forces of Juan Labaqui in the 1st battle of San Agustin del Palmar, taking 300 prisoners. Upon learning that the father of the victor, Leonardo Bravo, has been executed in Mexico City, Jose Maria Morelos orders the execution of the prisoners, but Bravo releases them.

13- Spain: the allies attack Retiro, the garrison commanded by Colonel Lefond surrenders, handing over his rifles, and 189 pieces of artillery, supplies and other equipment. The Spanish troops of Mendizabal temporarily enter Bilbao.

14 – Spain: French troops occupy Valladolid. United States: a group of Indian warriors attacked a column of civilians who had just evacuated Fort Dearborn escorted by some 70 soldiers. The result was a massacre, they killed more than fifty people and many others were captured to sell them as slaves to the British. These bought them to set them free, shortly after the British took Fort Dearborn. Meanwhile, General Sir Isaac Brock appeared before Detroit and demanded Hull to surrender. To intimidate him, he dressed his militiamen in British uniforms and insinuated that in case of an attack he could not prevent his Indian allies from committing all kinds of atrocities. The British began to bombard Detroit and, hearing the war cries of the Indians, against the opinion of their subordinates, Hull, who feared a massacre and had his daughter and grandson in the city, hoisted the white flag. The American militiamen were freed, while the regular soldiers were taken prisoner to Quebec. General Hull was brought before a council of war for the surrender of Detroit, and was sentenced to death, but will be pardoned by President Madison.

15 - Russia: Battle of Krasny; the Russians suffer 900 casualties, another 800 fall prisoners of the French.

16- Russia: Battle of Smolensk, the city, crossed by the Dnieper from east to west, is surrounded on its southern part by a sturdy stone and brick wall of 17 towers. General Raevsky has 13,000 soldiers and artillery in the square; to the north part of the 1st Western Army is deployed; the rest of this and the 2nd Bagration withdraw to Moscow. Napoleon arrives in the south, deploying troops from the Army Corps of Ney, Davout, Poniatowsky and Murat; the first two will attack the suburbs of the west and the center, while the cavalry of the others will try to wrap the city through the neighborhood outside the walls to the east. In total they have 50,000 French, Polish and Germans. The first skirmishes take place in the morning but the city resists. At night Raevsky is replaced by Doctorov, Barclay sends more reinforcements to the area and Bagration comes back with the intention of defending it, but it is two days away. In total there will be about 60,000 Russians in the area north of the river and in the square. After the failure of the first assault, the French deploy artillery batteries south of the city. Spain: 800 Swiss are surrendered in Guadalajara to Juan Martin "The Stubborn"

17- Russia: first match of Polotsk. At 04:00 in the morning, the French artillery begins to bomb the walls of Smolensk, until 5:00 p.m., the outer suburbs and some buildings of the interior are enveloped in flames, which had already been abandoned days before by the majority of its civil population. That morning, several Russian generals met with the President of the State Council, Marshal Saltikov, outside Smolensk, they agree that the critical Russian situation is due to the lack of coordination between their three armies, and the continuous withdrawal of Barclay inland, destroying property and property of the noble landowners proposing to the Tsar the general Kutuzov as the new commander-in-chief of all Russian armies. At dusk the cannonade was resumed sporadically in Smolensk, being answered by the Russian artillery. The French go on the assault, giving bloody street clashes in the suburbs of the city, taken by the French; but the 4 divisions of Doctorov retreat into the interior and continue their tenacious resistance.

18- Russia: at 02:00 in the morning, Barclay orders the bombing of the food and ammunition stores, ordering Doctorov to evacuate Smolensk by the north of the Dnieper, which he does after destroying the bridge of the river, thus setting the first great precedent of the Russian strategy of scorched earth. The French of Davout enter the interior of the ruined Smolensk around 04:00 hours, finding about 2,000 refugees inside the cathedral; then the Germans and Poles indulge in brutal sacking. Some 20,000 French were killed or injured; the Russians had about 14,000 casualties, many of them were already wounded from previous clashes and died while convalescing. Napoleon is desolate because the Russians have once again avoided a great battle, on the other hand, partisans and soldiers, sometimes alone, begin to harass their routes of supplies and communications, forcing him to allocate thousands of soldiers of his expedition to garrison populations, escort convoys and couriers. Smolensk will become a main base for his campaign to Moscow. Several Army Corps have been deployed in the rearguard to garrison occupied areas northwest of Russia. Among them are the 2nd, 6th, 7th, 9th and 10th Bodies of Oudinot, Saint Cyr, Renier, Victor and MacDonald and the men recruited in Lithuania; the Austrian Schwarzenberg Corps is sent to protect the right flank, southeast of Russia: in total more than 244,000 soldiers and their non-combatant personnel. Napoleon will be accompanied from this day by some 155,000 soldiers, the 1st, 3rd, 4th, 5th and 8th Army Corps of Davout, Ney, Eugene, Poniatowsky and Junot, to which the Imperial Guard and Reserve Cavalry Corps of Murat are added. In their wake they release the peasants from their servitude, in an attempt to turn them against their lords. The Grande Armée is already depleted by diseases and mass desertions, apart from casualties suffered in combat. Berthier and Caulaincuort will warn Bonaparte not to advance further by pursuing the Russian withdrawal, asking to stop the Grande Armée in Smolensk to reorganize it, solve its supply problems and consolidate the domain of the conquered territories. Napoleon ignores them, and again orders to march east to locate the Russian armies, in search of a decisive victory. The 1st and 2nd Russian armies under Barclay de Tolly and Bagration retreat to the east of Russia pursued by a large part of Napoleon's Grande Armée. The 3rd Corps of General Tuchkov arrives near Lubino, with the intention of protecting the Russian retreat by taking positions on the Stregan River, cutting off the Moscow road; in its direction the French vanguard approaches, the 3rd Corps of Marshal Ney. Spain: Arthur Wellesley obtains the title of Marques of Wellington. In Astorga 1,200 French are surrendered to the Spanish Colonel Eurile.

19 - Russia: battle of Valutina or Lubino: Tuchkov, with about 3,000 soldiers, orders to open fire with his batteries when the French approach. Ney stops his advance and orders to form a defensive line and deploy his artillery, while the 8th Junot Corps and the Murat cavalry arrive on their left flank; at 03:00 hours the French number 8,000 men. Bonaparte's plan consists of bagging the retreating Russian armies. Murat's cavalry tries to overtake Tuchkov on his left flank, but the 1st Russian cavalry corps of Orlov Denisov goes to the marshes and rejects the French riders. Murat asks for support from the Junot infantry, but his troops stop before a swamp. When Napoleon finds out in Smolensk, he says: "Junot lets the Russians escape ... I will lose the whole campaign because of him!" Ney's soldiers and artillery continue to press the Russian positions for the rest of the day, around the road to Moscow the struggle is constant, but the Russians defend themselves well and impede the passage of the French; both sides receive more reinforcements. At 9:00 p.m., the 3rd division of Davout's 1st Corps arrives at the front, Tuchkov sends the Ekaterinoslav Grenadier regiment against it. Napoleon even sent about 120,000 troops to the area, but largely due to Murat's failure and Junot's lack of support, the Western Armies of Barclay and Bagration manage to escape; which is another strategic failure for Bonaparte. When Ney interrupts his artillery fire, the Russian rear guard leaves Mount Valutino. The French had 10,000 casualties and the Russians about 15,000. During the fight, Tuchkov was wounded and captured; the French lost General Guden in combat.

20 - Russia: the Czar names Kutuzov as commander-in-chief of the Russian armies. United States: the American warship Constitution, under the command of Isaac Hull (brother of the incompetent General William Hull), encountered the English battleship Guerriere. After two and a half hours of cannon fire, the Guerriere was riddled and unserviceable.

22- Arabia: The Swiss explorer Jean Louis Burckhardt discovers the ancient city of Petra.

23- South America: before the advance of the royalists, the entire civilian population leaves Jujuy, blinding their wells and burning the crops, Belgrano, unknowingly imitating General Barclay, leaves the city with his army.

25 – Spain: end of the Cadiz Siege. With exceptionally well-planned fortifications, the garrison of the port city of Cadiz was in February 1810 2,000 soldiers, but was quickly reinforced by the Duke of Albuquerque with 10,000 more men, who worked improving their defenses, to turn the square into a bastion Impenetrable for the 60,000 French of Marshal Victor who besieged her since February 6 of that year. The Island of the Lion is where the Supreme Junta of Spain and the Indies retired as the French advanced on Seville a few days before arriving at Cadiz. In its port there is a British squadron, and 5,000 Englishmen are with the Spanish garrison. Today Marshal Victor decides to withdraw the rest of his troops before the allies surround him.

26- South America: Simon Bolivar leaves Venezuela for the island of Curaçao, very close to the Venezuelan coast, but under British rule.

27 - Spanish troops liberate Seville.

28- South America: the Mbayas Indians, allied with the Portuguese and equipped with Portuguese firearms, occupy the Bourbon Fort, which was soon returned by the Portuguese to the government of Paraguay, whose dictator reinforces it and renames Fort Olympus.

29 – Spain: French troops occupy Bilbao.

31- Spain: Joseph Bonaparte retires through the Tagus to Valencia.

SEPTEMBER-1812

1 – South America: the Peruvian army of Tristan invades Jujuy and enters Salta.

2- Spain: Wellington leaves Madrid. United States: a horde of Indians attacks the town of Pigeon Roost, in the territory of Indiana, where they kill twenty-four settlers, including fifteen children. Two other children were kidnapped, the event was known as the Pigeon Roost massacre. South America: José Miguel Carrera assumes dictatorial powers in Chile and O'Higgins confronts him.

3- Russia: the Russians stop their withdrawal and take positions in the Borodino plain. To the north of the plain runs the Kolocha River, from east to west, several tributaries flow to the south: the Voinak, Semenovka, Kamenka and the Stonets. To the south passes the Old Smolensk Road to Moscow, about 120 km away. And further south is the forest of Outitza. South America: the vanguard of Tristan reaches the rear of Belgrano next to the river of the Stones and a fight is fought in which the Peruvians were put to flight with many casualties. After this skirmish, Belgrano decides that, instead of heading to Córdoba according to the orders received, it would be better to take refuge in Tucumán.

4- Russia: Barclay de Tolly, commanding the Russian army until the arrival of Kutuzov, positions troops and builds trenches in the hills from the northeast bank of the Kolocha to this forest, passing through eastern Borodino, in a line of about 8 km length from north to south, thus completely closing the route to Moscow. On the northeast bank of the Kolocha, where the arrival of the French is expected, the three Maslovsky forts rise, armed with 26 cannons. In Gorki, northwest of Borodino, 12 more pieces are positioned on a hill. To the southeast of Borodino the Great Redoubt of General Raevsky is built on a hill, in the form of "V", located in the center of the Russian deployment and armed with 26 guns. Barclay de Tolly deploys his 1st Western Army northeast of Borodino, to the right of the Russian deployment, consisting of the Cossacks of Platov, the 1st Cavalry Corps of Ouvarov, the 2nd and 4th Corps of Baggovout Army and Osterman to the northeast of Gorky ; and the 2nd Cavalry Corps commanded by Korf. The right flank is the strongest sector of the Russian order, commanding by General Milordarovich. From Gorky to the Great Redoubt, north of the Russian center is the 6th Corps of Docturov. Bagration deploys its 2nd Western Army from the Great Redoubt to the forests of Outiza. The fort is guarded by troops of the 7th Army Corps of Raevsky, deployed to the forts of Bagration further south; after him they form the 3rd and 4th Cavalry Corps, Pahlen and Sievers. Prince Gorchakov commands the left flank, behind the Semenovkaya, whose town is dismantled to deploy 24 artillery pieces. The sector is defended by the 8th Borozdine Army Corps. On the left wing 3 fortifications are erected under the command of General Bagration himself, in the form of "V"; two in front and one behind, this is hidden from the enemy's view. A mile to the west in front of these forts is the redoubt of Schwardino or Shevardino; as Barclay waits for the French in the north, its deployment on the entire southern flank is much weaker than after Borodino and the northeast of the Kolocha River. In the rear, in the center of the Russian deployment, they form two divisions of Cuirassiers and the 5th Imperial Guard Corps of Prince Constantine and the 3rd Tuchkov Army Corps, in addition to 300 field cannons; this is the Russian Reserve. Spain: Spanish troops liberate Córdoba.

5- Russia: Napoleon arrives in the morning at Valuevo, 2 km east of Borodino, checking that the Russian formations are closed, vulnerable to artillery, and that their reserves are too close to the front. The lookouts of the fort of Shevardino give the alarm to the proximity of Murat and Poniatowsky, who have fought combat with Russian units making them retreat; Eugene approaches by the north of Valuevo. Bonaparte deploys the bulk of his troops to the southwest of Borodino, orders the 5th Corps of Poniatowski to flank the Russian left and sends the 5th Division of General Compass to assault Shevardino fort. General Gorchakov places a division of cuirassiers behind Shevardino, garrisoned by an infantry division and 12 cannons, sends three regiments of hunters to the ravine of the town of Doronino, to ambush the French vanguard, and sends a force of Cossacks to the Old Way of Smolensk, to intercept Poniatowski. Midmorning, the Compans division attacks Shevardino with the 1st and 2nd Cavalry Corps. After 2 hours of artillery duel and fusillade discharges, they advance towards Doronino and the nearby forests, while in Yelnia, Poniatowski expels the Russian infantrymen; his Dragons and Hussars counterattack chasing away the Poles, but in Shevardino they begin to retreat despite receiving reinforcements from Bagration. At 7:00 p.m., two French regiments take the fort and an hour later they invade the town in a pincer maneuver, dislodging the defenders with 4-gun shrapnel fire and a subsequent bayonet assault. At 21:00 hours, Gorchakov counterattacks with Borozdin's 8th Corps, which recovers the redoubt after a bloody assault, while the Cuirassiers push back the French columns. After several discussions between Bagration and Gorchakov at dusk, they decide to evacuate the semi-destroyed fort at around 11:00 p.m. At night the French continue attacking, while the Russians retreat in good order protected by Cuirassiers; finally the French take the position of Shevardino. In total the French launched three divisions, some 35,000 soldiers; the Russians came to employ some 18,000 men in Shevardino's defense. Each of the two sides would lose some 8,000 soldiers in this impromptu battle; the Russians offered tenacious resistance and none were captured alive.

6 - Russia: General Mihail Kutozov arrives in Borodino and assumes the command of the Russian armies, some 120,000 soldiers, 20,000 militiamen and 640 cannons, relieving Barclay de Tolly, who nevertheless remains in command of the 1st Western Army. Kutuzov reorganizes the command of the fronts of the Russian army and Orders the 3º Body of Tuchkov, in reserve, to position itself to the south of the forts of Bagration, to try to flank any enemy force that arrived by the Old Smolensk Road; the general does not make more changes in the initial deployment and is limited to wait for the arrival of the bulk of the French armies, which surprises many of his officers. In the morning, Napoleon examines the Russian positions, planning while his troops arrive. Ney and Murat propose to attack immediately by the ravine of Semenovskaya, to cut the Russian deployment, but Bonaparte refuses to not have enough men yet. He decides to make his main attack on the Russian southern center while flanking his left wing along the Old Smolensk Road. Another secondary attack will go to Borodino. Russian positions northeast of the Kolocha will be ignored. For the main assault, it has on its right wing, south of Shevardino, Davout's 1st Army Corps, some 85,000 soldiers, supported by the 1st, 2nd and 4th Cavalry Corps commanded by Nansouty, Mountbrun and Lateur Mabourg. The 5th Corps of Poniatowski will attempt the flanking by the Old Way. However, Napoleon is unaware that there is a third Russian fort behind which he can see. In the French center the 8th and 3rd Corps of Junot and Ney are located, which will attack Semenovska and the Bagration forts. On the French left, to the north, are the 4th Corps of Eugene and the 3rd Cavalry Corps of Grouchy, on the north bank of the Kolocha. They must take Borodino and then attack the Raevsky Redoubt. Behind it forms the French Reserve: the cavalry of the Imperial Guard of Bessiéres, the artillery of the Guard of Sorbier, the Young Guard of Lobau and behind the Old Guard of Mortier, next to Napoleon, whose position of command is near Shevardino, Murat send the cavalry Reserve; In total, the French gather about 130,000 men and 587 guns at the end of the day. Kutuzov inspects the positions of his army, giving full freedom of tactical decision to his generals before the approaching battle; which means that he delegates the command to Barclay and Bagration. Order the artillerymen to shoot the enemy when they are at their practical reach and predict to the infantry that the use of the bayonet will be crucial. In the afternoon, Russian engineers reinforce General Raevsky's Redoubt with wood obtained from dismantling several villages, digging a deep ditch and bringing more campaign pieces, until protecting it with some 200 guns in the vicinity, although the French can see only their battery of 26 pieces. Meanwhile, Napoleon is informed of the defeat of Marmont before the Marquis of

Wellington in Salamanca, which occurred on the 22nd of last July. Despite this, he continues to give orders to his marshals about the maneuvers and objectives of tomorrow. Bonaparte orders that at dawn the artillery of the 1st Corps attack the redoubts of Bagration with 72 guns before assaulting them; another redoubt must be bombarded with 40 pieces before the assault of the 3rd and 7th Bodies. Poniatowsky will try to flank the Russian left wing on the south road. Troops of the 4th Corps of Eugene shall take Borodino, and the Morand divisions and Gerard shall assault Raevsky's Great Redoubt.

7 - Russia: **Battle of Borodino**, Napoleon rides to Shevardino Hill, where he watches the sunrise at 05:30 am, predicting: "- The sun is bright, it's like the sun of Austerlitz" Half an hour later, all his soldiers are in formation, awaiting orders. At 06:30 hours, the 102 cannons of Davout open fire; but the positions of Borozdin's 8th Corps are out of reach; On the other hand, the Ney salvos reach the northernmost basin of Bagration. The troops of the 4th Corps of Eugene advance towards Borodino, with the division of Delzon in vanguard, they push to the regiments of Russian hunters and the reinforcements that Barclay sends them to the other side of the Kolocha; most are massacred when they cross the bridge, shot at close range by the French, who then advance towards Gorky. Towards 07:00 hours, the 6th Corps of Docturov counterattacks, pushing Dolzon back to Borodino, and flying the bridge. Eugene sends the divisions of Gerard and Broussier to the front, Grouchy's 3rd Cavalry Corps and an artillery battery to support the attack on Raevsky's Great Redoubt. From now on, the confrontation is divided into six different scenarios along the front and the day: the Forts of Bagration, the village of Semenovska, Borodino, the Great Redoubt of Raevsky, and the Old Smolensk Way. Resolved the fights in these places, the combats begin to decline until their cessation. Towards 07:00 hours, the 1st Corps of Davout attacks the redoubts of Bagration supported by troops of the 5th of Poniatowsky and 30 guns of Sorbier. Comapans, general of the French division at the forefront of the attack, is wounded and relieved by Dessaix; Davout himself is unconscious. A strong fire from the forts makes the French go back, being persecuted by the 4th Corps of Russian Cavalry of Sievers. Another French division initiates a second assault, also being rejected.

At 09:00 the 1st Corps of Davout launches a third assault, with the division of Ledru, supported by troops of the 8th Corps of Junot and the 1st and 4th Cavalry Corps; Raevsky, Constantin and Tuchkov send Granaderos, regiments of the Russian Imperial Guard and Cuirassiers, who reject the French, but Bagration is mortally wounded at 09:45, being relieved by Raevsky. At 10:00 hours, Ledru launches a fourth round taking one of the forts, but is expelled by the division of Konownitzin supported by Hussars and Dragons. Murat orders a battalion of German hunters and a French infantry regiment a counterattack, but the Russian cuirassiers surround them; the division of Wurttemberg comes to their aid and allows them to retire. Around 11:00 am, some 26,000 Frenchmen storm the forts defended by 18,000 Russians from Ravesky. Napoleon orders the 5th of Poniatowski to collaborate in the attack, but Borozdin's 8th Corps makes them retreat again, supported by the regiment of Reserve Grenadiers; the French regroup and counterattack for the sixth time, giving a fierce battle for the redoubts. At 11:30 in the morning the French finally conquer the forts of Bagration; Konovnitzin withdraws his troops behind the Semenovskaya ravine. In the battle for these fortifications the French have employed a total of 45,000 soldiers and 400 cannons; the Russians employed fewer men, and used about 300 cannons.

After the capture of the town of Borodino, Eugene orders three divisions of his 4th Army Corps to attack the Great Redoubt and take it. But its slowness of maneuver induces the Russian generals to believe that it is a distraction, and they move troops from the center to the strongholds of Bagration, to the south, which are being attacked from 07:00 hours; but then Ney redirects his artillery against the Redoubt and surroundings, followed by Eugene's. At

09:45 in the morning, the divisions of Morand, Gerard and Broussier, cross the Kolocha by pontoons. Raevsky's 7th Corps troops repel a French reconnaissance force; by then Bagration is seriously wounded further south, and Raevsky takes command of the entire 2nd Western Army, ordering the Russian division of Konovnitzin to advance to the central front. At 10:00 hours the division of Morand advances towards the Great Redoubt, defended by the 7th Russian Army Corps with 26 pieces of artillery. The French scatter the hunters of the Semenovskaya River and take it after defeating their garrison. The regiment of Yermolov and the 3rd Kreutz Cavalry Corps counter-attack and stop the French offensive. Barclay sends two more Russian divisions, the French escape before being surrounded, but the Russian hunters find a group inside, annihilating it. Koutaissof, the main artillery general of the 1st Russian Army, is killed in the action. Around 11:00, the French are coming back for assault for the second time. The 3rd Corps of French cavalry attacks the division of Prince Von Wurttemberg, which forms a frame, and suffers many losses until the riders of Kreutz and the regiment of Yermolov push back the French again. The French offensive in the sector stagnates. Napoleon orders to place 170 cannons on the central front, which will bombard the Great Redoubt area for the next two hours, removing its palisades, embankments and ditches, losing part of its defensive capacity, although it still retains its artillery and garrison.

The center of the French lines, from the Great Redoubt to the village of Semenovskaya, will be defended during the following 3 hours by the 4th Cavalry Corps of Lateur Maubourg and Carabineros of the 2nd Corps. The Russian artillery causes havoc among them, Montbrun, the commander of the latter, is killed, replaced by Caulaincourt. At 2:00 pm, Napoleon orders Eugene to resume the attack on the Great Redoubt, and this sends to the divisions of Broussieres, Gerard and Morand, supported by the cavalry division of Chastel and two other divisions of Cuirassiers. Barclay orders Ostermann, of the 4th Russian Corps, to retreat to a new line east of the Redoubt, backed by the 7th of Raevsky, two regiments of the Imperial Guard, and the 2nd and 3rd Cavalry Corps of Korf and Pahlen, but these do not they come to occupy their positions. The French, Saxon, Polish and Westphalian riders carry a charge under the fire of the Great Redoubt artillery and the Russian infantry lines. Three divisions of cavalry are shot with closed firings at less than 60 steps or swept by cannon fire and shrapnel.

The Saxons assault the northern parapet of the Redoubt, many being eliminated by Russian bayonets, whose infantry raise their rifles forming a bristling barrier. The 4th Cavalry Corps of Lateur Maubourg is sent to attack. Finally the French, Polish and Westphalian riders enter the fort, locking up a fierce, chaotic and terribly bloody hand-to-hand combat, they do not take prisoners. Behind the cavalry, the divisions of French infantry arrive at the Great Redoubt, conquering it at 3:00 p.m. The Russians retire, and in spite of the bloody fight, they were able to take 6 cannons; that loss is the retreat of the Russian center, but his determined defense has caused many casualties to Napoleon. On the Russian right, northeast of the Kolocha, the Cossack horse commander Platov finds a ford to cross the river and ride to the southwest, to release the French pressure on the Great Redoubt, attacked at this time by troops of the 4th Corps of Eugene. Kutuzov approves the flanking operation. At 11:00 in the morning, the Cossacks of Platov and the 1st Cavalry Corps of General Ouvarov with 12 cannons, cross the Kolocha, fighting northeast of Borodino with a French regiment supported by a brigade of light Bavarian and Italian cavalry. The Russians carry out three charges but are rejected; then they open fire with their artillery, forcing the French to retreat. At noon, the feared Russian horsemen find in Borodino the fierce resistance of the division of Delzon, supported by the Bavarian and Italian horsemen; In addition, a brigade of the 3rd Cavalry Corps of Grouchy, who carries out a deadly charge against the Russians, comes to his aid. Napoleon himself observes danger on his left flank and sends his Imperial Guard and the Vistula Legion to the south of

Borodino. Before the arrival of more French riders and their elite reinforcements, the Cossacks beat in retreat towards the Kolocha at around 2:00 p.m. His withdrawal is blamed for cowardice by the Russian officialdom; that he will also reproach Kutuzov for refusing to send reinforcements. Actually Napoleon commanded up to 16 of Grouchy's regiments and his precious Guard to this front, concentrating his attention on him until 3:00 p.m. While maintaining the assaults on the Redoubts of Bagration and Raevsky, Napoleon ordered another attack to the south of the Russian center in Semenovska, preceded by a bombardment, with Saxon troops of the 1st and 3rd Army Corps and the 1st and 4th Cavalry Corps. The town is defended by a division of Grenadiers, two regiments of the Russian Guard, a division of Cuirassiers and several artillery batteries. At 10:00 hours, the Saxon charge, under the fire of the Russian artillery, crosses the river Semenovskaya, breaks the picture of the division of Grenadiers and enters the town attacking the Guard formed in six squares, which counterattacks carrying the bayonet with its Cuirassiers. The Saxons flee, covered by Friant's infant division, which scatters the Russian horsemen with the help of Westphalian Cuirassiers. At 11:00 hours, the division of Russian Grenadiers stops the Semenovska River the advance of the division of Friant, which retreats. Murat requires him to counterattack, expel the Grenadiers, taking the town and opening a breach in the Russian deployment. But the exhausted French do not have more troops in the sector to continue. Murat and Ney ask Napoleon to send them to the Young Guard to penetrate the Russian rear, but he refuses. At noon, General Beillard repeats the request, in vain, because Bonaparte does not want to risk his reserves. The Russians take advantage to flee to the forests after the Semenovskaya. To plug the breach, Barclay sends the 4th Corps of Ostermann-Tolstoy, which until now had been idle north of the Great Redoubt. Napoleon sends Sorbier to the front with 60 cannons, which bombard the 4th Corps during its advance. Ostermann's soldiers receive shocks that sweep entire platoons. Finally they stop to the east of the Great Redoubt, supporting during the next 5 hours the heavy French bomber, which will cause thousands of casualties; the Russians will limit themselves to withdraw the dead and wounded to take their place.

At 08:00 hours, in the south of the forts of Bagration, the 5th Corps of Poniatowsky, which was trying to flank the Russian 2nd Western Army by the Old Smolensk Road, is stopped by the fire of a division of Grenadiers of the 3rd Corps of Tuchkov, stationed in the hills of Utitza with 36 cannons and Muscovite militiamen. From 10:30 in the morning, Poniatowski bombs them with 22 guns. Kutuzov orders Baggovout, idle to the northeast of the Kolocha, to direct his 2nd Army Corps three miles south to reinforce Tuchkov, leaving six regiments of hunters in the Kolocha in case the French intend to outflank the 1st Western Army from the north. At noon, the 2nd and 3rd Russian Army Corps advance through the town of Utitza, being counterattacked by the Poles. Tuchkov himself falls dead, and General Pavlov takes charge of his troops, later Baggovout assumes command of the entire southern Russian flank.

At 3:00 p.m. Poniatowski's artillery ceases fire, the Polish column advancing north of Mount Utitza meets troops of the 2nd Russian Corps supported by four militia regiments; but the main Polish attack is carried out south of Mount Utitza. Baggovout counterattacks with the Cossacks of Karpov, a division of Grenadiers and another division of Russian infantry, but they can't contain the Poles. Baggavout decides to withdraw all his 2nd Corps towards the east of the Old Smolensko Road, and the withdrawal drags the 3rd Corps fighting south, leaving Monte Utitza in the hands of Poniatowski, who sends four cavalry regiments in pursuit of the Russians, but Karpov's Cossacks reject him. The entire southern front of the 2nd Russian Western Army retreats to the northeast, with Prince Eugene of Wurttemberg covering his retreat. The Russians form another line further east that cuts the Old Smolensk Road. Kutozov's staff receives the bad news of the retreat of his left flank. Some will accuse the general of lack of foresight of a French attack from the south, sending scant reinforcements there in the morning.

Napoleon's army has advanced from Borodino and the Great Redoubt, to the north, passing through Semenovskaya, to the forests of Outiza to the south. Deploy, from north to south, the 4th Corps of Eugene on its left flank, the 3rd of Ney, and the 1st of Davout in its center, and the 8th of Junot and the 5th of Poniatowsky on its right flank. The Imperial Guard, some 20,000 men, continues in Schewardino, where Bonaparte is. Kutuzov, on the other hand, has disregarded the progress of the battle, delegating to his officers. Barclay, who holds the tactical command, informs him that the Russian deployment is very compromised: his troops have retreated and the last remaining fortified stronghold is north of its center, in Gorky, about 2 km northeast of Borodino. Kutozov orders to form a new front line 1,000 steps east of the lost Great Redoubt, from Gorky, through the villages of Kniaskowo and Psarewo to the forest of Outiza. He intends to resist until the night, and then gather more reinforcements and continue the fight tomorrow. His soldiers are exhausted, hungry and have suffered thousands of casualties; but he believes that Napoleon's army is in similar conditions. Barclay withdraws to the east the entire center line and the left wing of the front of the Russian 1st Western Army; forming with the 6th and 4th Army Corps of Doctorov and Ostermann a powerful concave line, reinforced behind by the remains of the 7th Raevsky Corps and two regiments of the Russian Imperial Guard. In the north, on its right flank, the Cossacks and four regiments of hunters are located on the northeast bank of the Kolocha. But to the south, the center line of the 2nd Western Army has retreated 1 km, formed by the 8th Corps of Borozdin and the 2nd Corps of Baggavout, and up to 2 km on its left flank, where the 3rd Corps is, now also at command of Baggavout. In the Reserve remains the 5th Corps of Constantine, a part of the Guard and regiments of Lithuanian hunters; in total about 5,000 soldiers, less than the French Reserve. At 16:00 hours, Barclay attacks the Great Redoubt with a Russian division, but retreats before the counterattack of a Polish Cuirassiers brigade. On the other hand, the French launch loads of cavalry against the center and the Russian left, but the infants of the 3º and 4º Bodies make them retire when forming impregnable pictures. In the area southeast of the Great Redoubt, the riders of Generals Defrance, Chastel, and Houssaye, reinforced by troops of the 5th Corps of Poniatowski, undo two pictures of a Russian division taking their artillery. Two regiments of cavalry counterattack the Saxons and Poles making them flee, recovering the lost cannons, and giving them back machine-gun the 4th Corps of French cavalry, making them retreat, while the 2nd Corps of Russian cavalry attacked the divisions of Wathier and Defrance. The attacks and counterattacks follow, converting the area southeast of the Redoubt into a continuous duel of cavalry, raising a large cloud of dust that covers the sector.

At 5:00 pm the cavalry fight loses intensity. The infantry and horsemen of both sides are already physically exhausted, but the mutual artillery bombardment will continue until nightfall. Around 6:00 p.m. personal combat begins to decline until it ceases completely. At that time, Kutuzov's staff began to fear that Napoleon would send his Guard to the front, undamaged and willing to act, but when his staff asked Bonaparte for the third time to send her to fight, he replied: "- No I will see my Guard destroyed ... 800 leagues from France I will not risk my last reservation .... "This repeated refusal to send the Guard to the front will be criticized by its officers. Kutuzov sends an ambiguous report to Alexander I, saying that his powerful artillery has caused many casualties to Napoleon, forcing him to retreat. Tsar will rise to Marshal.

In fact, some Russian divisions have been reduced to regiments; in the 7th Division there are only 700 soldiers; many battalions have no more than 200 left. Of the six Grenadier battalions that fought in the Bagration forts, only 300 men remain; to the Regiment of Cuirassiers of the Zarina only 95 horsemen remain. At 21:00 hours at night, the Russians, decimated, exhausted, hungry, thirsty, and still harassed by the French artillery, begin to retreat to the east. The floats that can still roll are used to evacuate the wounded by abandoning the ammunition and tools they carried. Kutozov will justify the withdrawal to the Tsar claiming that it is a tactical retreat to a new position in the heights of Mozhaisk.

The French, although they have not suffered so many casualties; they are not in a position to pursue the Russian withdrawal by pure physical exhaustion. Napoleon has been very depressed; he has not achieved his goal: some 60,000 Russians are retired, and will receive more reinforcements and supplies to be in their homeland, while he must move further from their sources of supply to beat them, and the relentless Russian winter inexorably approaches. The Russians have lost some 60,000 soldiers, including 23 generals, such as Bagration; they left behind 20 guns and about 20,000 cannon balls. The French suffer 30,000 casualties, 43 generals, among them Montbrun, and 110 colonels; that add to the 150,000 soldiers that have lost in the Russian campaign to this day. During the battle, the French fired some 60,000 cannon shots. For Napoleon it is a tactical victory, but the strategic triumph is Kutuzov.

In Spain: Wellington marches to meet General Claussel after leaving three divisions on the Tagus; then Claussel leaves Valladolid retiring to Burgos.

Borodino is the bloodiest battlefield of military history until the 20th century.

9 – Russia: combat of Mozhaisk.

10 - Combat of Krimskoïe, Russian Partisans liberate the city of Verea; 300 French die

11- United States: General Harrison had been commissioned to help Fort Harrison and Fort Wayne. He sent a detachment of 1,000 men to the first and he himself marched towards the second. They arrived this morning and, in both cases, the Indians left without offering resistance. Harrison ordered the arrest of Captain Rhea. Subsequently, a commission of inquiry will be convened, but Rhea will be allowed to present his resignation out of respect for his years of service. The fact that the Indian attacks on the forts were rejected caused many warriors to lose confidence in their chiefs and to join the ranks of Tecumseh. During the following months Harrison will send diverse games to avenge the Indian attacks and killings. In most of them, the American soldiers will devastate numerous Indian villages, often evacuated before they arrive, although in others they will be ambushed and will have to flee.

12 - Russian General Bagration dies, wounded in Borodino. Mexico: Leonardo Bravo, one of the lieutenants of the Mexican insurgent José María Morelos, had been captured along with some of his men and taken to Mexico City, where he had been sentenced to death. Morelos proposed to Viceroy Venegas to exchange him for the Spaniards captured in Cuautla, but tonight Bravo and his followers were executed. Upon hearing the news, Morelos proposed Bravo's son to kill the Spanish hostages, but he chose to release them.

13- South America: the Portuguese government of Rio de Janeiro accepted the Rademaker-Herrera treaty, mainly because the British ambassador had informed a few days before he had British authorization to take the measures he deemed necessary for it to be fulfilled. Soon after, Diogo de Sousa evacuated his soldiers from the Banda Oriental. However, some border territories that until the invasion had been Spanish remained since then under Portuguese sovereignty. On the other hand, Belgrano arrived in Tucumán with the Jujeños, where he found a population willing to help him with men, money and supplies. Tristan's army moved more slowly, for it only found scorched earth in its path.

14- The Russian columns retreating from the west began to arrive in Moscow, being received with expectation by the population, who contemplates desolate as his soldiers cross the avenues in silence, with their heads down, and then leave through the other side of the city in address to Bronnitsy. The bulk of the Russian army is stationed in the vicinity of Panky, about 15 km southeast of Moscow.

15- Russia: At 5:00 p.m., a Russian War Council is held in Phili, to discuss the advisability of leaving Moscow, a situation that is hated by generals such as Barclay, Osterman-Tolstoy and Raevsky. After listening to them, Kutuzov finally decides to conserve his army, ordering to sacrifice the capital to save the rest of Russia. This decision displeases many, Barclay will resign from the army, but the Tsar will ask for his return in December.

16- Russia: That morning when the Russian rear guard withdrew from Moscow by the Yauza river bridge, the French army's vanguard, a cavalry unit commanded by Murat, entered the capital through the Dorogomilov gate. The Russian soldiers offered a desperate resistance, the general Miloradovich still maintains in the city two Cavalry Corps, ten regiments of Cossacks and 12 cannons. In the same way as in Smolensk, Kutuzov orders the destruction of ammunition and supply depots. The Moscow governor, Rostopchin, frees prisoners from prisons, which are immediately engaged in looting, when the first fires begin to emerge, water pumps are dismantled by Russian officials. Groups of looters and saboteurs attack the French firing from windows and roofs with a thousand rifles that have been delivered by the Russian army. Milordarovich tells Murat that, if he does not allow him to retreat, his soldiers will defend the city street by street and house by house, Murat gives him four hours to finish the evacuation and capitulate. At midday, Napoleon arrives at the hill of Poklonnaya, in sight of Moscow, there awaits the arrival of a Russian envoy with the keys of the capital, as a gesture of surrender, but it will be in vain. The Muscovites collect their belongings, and continue the withdrawal of their army in long caravans that fill the doors and bridges: of the 250,000 citizens, only about 15,000 will remain in the capital, almost all sick and wounded soldiers. The small colony of French and their allies decides to remain in the city for obvious reasons.
At 3:00 p.m., when Napoleon triumphantly enters Moscow spectacularly escorted by his Imperial Guard to the tune of the Marseillaise, he is astonished to find the empty avenues; enters the Kremlin and climbs to the tower of Ivan the Great from which he contemplates the whole apparently lifeless city. With the seizure of the capital he hoped that Tsar Alexander would submit to his rulings, and for that purpose he would send a letter to St. Petersburg. Bonaparte declares Moscow as a war trophy and authorizes his troops to plunder, as he promised at the beginning of the campaign. Except for the Kremlin and the churches, several hundred Muscovite wooden houses belong to very rich nobles. The looting is organized until September 19: today the Old Guard will do it, tomorrow, the Young Guard, the day after, Davout Army Corps. However, the order to stop it will be ignored, killing and increasing the number of fires. At dusk Moscow is engulfed in flames, burning entire neighborhoods that threaten the Kremlin. United States: A supply party marching toward Fort Harrison was the victim of an ambush by the Potawatomi Indians. Then the Potawatomi left the area and this afternoon attacked the house of a settler named Hudson, who was absent, but they killed his wife and their four children in what was known as the Prairie Lamotte massacre.

17 – Napoleon leaves the Kremlin this morning, to stay at the Palace of Peter the Great, where he will stay for three days. This afternoon the wind changes direction and the whole city is clouded by smoke, the Old Guard has saved the Kremlin by digging a ditch around it; The neighborhood of the Kuznetzky Bridge was also protected by a unit of Grenadiers assisted by the foreigners' colony that resides in the capital. The Württemberg soldiers plunder the cathedral of Arkhangelsk, Blagoveshensk and the Kremlin itself, coming to desecrate tombs of tsars and all series of orthodox relics. Spain: Spanish troops liberate Granada.

18- Spain: The allies besiege Burgos with two infantry divisions and 8 pieces of artillery, while the other troops are quartered in Monasterio. Russia: after withdrawing from Moscow and while the French are plundering it, the Russian army under Kutuzov retreats to the southeast by the Ryazan road, crosses the Moscow River by Borovsky and turns west; arriving this afternoon to Podolsk. Napoleon sends Murat, Bessieres and the Poles of Poniatowsky in their search, but Miloradovich dispatches Cossacks in various directions to mislead them. The French ignore where the 100,000 Russians have withdrawn.

19 – Russia: in Moscow the fires begin to lose strength when it begins to rain and the wind abates. The fire and the sacking of Moscow will be crossed out in all Europe as an act of barbarism that discredits Bonaparte, and will be a blow to Russian morals. The French will remain in the capital until October, for about 35 days. Spain: begins the site of the Castle of Burgos: the French reinforce the castle and establish a bastion 250 meters north of the castle. Wellington decides not to wait for the arrival of the rest of his artillery train and orders an assault on the bastion, which is conquered during the night at the cost of 500 allied casualties; the defenders retreat to the castle.

20 – Russia: in Nesvizh, the Cossack cavalry defeat three French squadrons.

21 - South America: the first national flag of Paraguay comes in use with colors inspired by the French tricolor.

22 - Spain: That night Wellington ordered to cross the moat and climb the wall of the castle, about 23 feet high. The French repel the assault causing many casualties, and the allies begin to dig a tunnel from the bastion.
 Russia: in Vishnyakovka, Russian Partisans capture a detachment of 500 Frenchmen looking for supplies.

23 - South America: by order of the First Triumvirate, Belgrano moves from Jujuy to Tucumán (Argentina), and with just 1,800 men defeats the 3,000 royalists of Pio Tristan at the Battle of Tucumán. Tristan had left without permission of his boss Goyeneche in pursuit of the Argentine Juan José Castelli, his defeat left Goyeneche unprotected by the south and forces him to retreat and entrench himself in Salta.

24 – Russia: in Vyazma, Russian Partisans massacre a French detachment. South America: Tristan arrives in Tucumán and is intercepted by the army of Belgrano in battle formation.

25 - South America: Battle of Tucumán, the action develops quite disorganized and a huge cloud of locusts increased the prevailing chaos, the Peruvians withdraw to Salta leaving numerous casualties, weapons, ammunition and provisions.

26 - Russia: Kutuzov resumed the march towards the south, towards Tarutino, while detachments of Partisans, Cossacks and Hussars harassed the French permanently. Lieutenant Colonel Davidov commands the first regular unit of this type, consisting of 50 Cossacks and 80 Hussars, attacking the garrisons, couriers, supply convoys and patrols of the invaders with great success, demoralizing them. To complete this strategy, 500 rifles are distributed among peasants to take action as guerrillas.

 27 - Russia: Kutuzov camps in Tarutino awaiting the arrival of troops, weapons and supplies, thanks to his skillful maneuver, Kutuzov saves Kaluga and Tula, where troops and armaments are concentrated, reestablishes communications with the armies of Tormasov and Chichagov, and at the same time It cuts Napoleon's supply routes to Smolensk and southern Russia, being encamped southwest of Moscow, where the French have enormous shortages of supplies.

28 - Battle of Tarutino, General Bennigsen defeats the cavalry of Murat, who manages to escape the annihilation thanks to the timely intervention of Poniatowsky.

29 - South America: the Argentine Cornelio Zelaya beats the royalist José Domingo Vidart in the 2nd battle of the Río de las Piedras, in Salta.

30 - Ottoman Empire: coronation of the Grand vizier Kursit Pacha.

OCTOBER-1812

1- Spain: French troops take the castle of Chinchilla.

2- Russia: if it does not get supplies, Bonaparte will have to give up its plans to arrive in Saint Petersburg this year and it will even be impossible to continue the campaign to the interior of Russia, where the temperature begins to fall gradually.

3- Russia: For the past two weeks, the majority of the Grande Armée has been locked on the defensive with Napoleon in Moscow, only about 26,000 soldiers under Murat are deployed outside, on the banks of the Chernisnya, stationed between the villages of Teterinka and Dmitrovskoe, southwest of the city. In front of them, about 6 km away, they are watched by the vanguard of the Russian army.

4- Spain: Wellington exploits the tunnel, opening a breach in the walls of the castle of Burgos; soon the allies occupy the courtyard and begin to organize the next assault on the castle.

5- South America: Juan José Castelli had returned to Buenos Aires, where a trial had been opened for his performance in Upper Peru, although it was not clear what the accusations against him were. A tongue cancer made his defense difficult, until he died tonight with the trial still open.

6- South America: the Argentine Cornelio Zelaya is defeated in Jujuy by the royalist colonel Indalecio Gonzalez Socasa. In Mexico the freedom of the press enshrined in the new Constitution is proclaimed and the writer Jose Joaquin Fernandez de Lizardi founded in the city the radical liberal newspaper "The Mexican thinker".

7- United States: the American ship Wasp captures the British Frolic off the coast of Virginia.

8- South America: The victory of Beltrano in Tucumán had occurred despite the insistence of the triumvirate to not present battle, and this made the popularity of the triumvirs decline. This morning Jose de San Martin and Francisco Ortiz de Ocampo, with the help of the Lautaro Lodge and the Patriotic Society, gathered their troops in the main square and forced the holding of elections to elect a new triumvirate and a constituent assembly. The new triumvirs were Juan Jose Paso, Nicolas Rodriguez Peña and Antonio Alvarez Jonte; they will rule dominated by the Lautaro Lodge.

9 – Russia: in Nickolaevka, Russian Partisans kill 100 French and capture 200. South America: the Royal Squadron of 5 ships of Captain Manuel Montverde sacks San Nicolas de los Arroyos, near Buenos Aires, and with the reinforcement of three ships leave course to Rosario.

10- South America: Chilean dictator José Miguel Carrera had sent agents to Concepción that destabilized the government of Juan Martinez de Rozas. A popular revolt had dissolved the Junta de Concepción and had arrested its members. Rozas was taken to Santiago de Chile and Carrera exiled him to Mendoza. There he was received with public honors. This career policy won supporters to the royalists of Concepcion. In Valdivia, the army was placed under the orders of the Viceroy of Peru.

11- Spain, in Burgos the Dubreton troops made several exits by surprise, and managed to delay the work of English sappers causing some casualties. The rainy weather makes it even more difficult to delay their works more than they should.

12- Russia: the Cossacks and Partisans roam everywhere observing all French maneuvers in search of any weakness, attacking small units and capturing prisoners and deserters.

13- United States: Americans crossed the Niagara to invade Canada. The Niagara flows from south to north communicating Lake Erie with Lake Ontario, the east bank corresponds to the State of New York, while the western one is Canadian. The US army consisted of some 6,000 men under the command of General Stephen van Ressenlaer. The British had detected the preparations for the invasion and General Brock was willing to face it. The fight was fought in Queenston Heights, and the British won a resounding victory. The Americans counted 100 dead, 300 wounded and almost a thousand prisoners. Van Ressenlaer resigned after the battle. Nevertheless, Brock died during the combat, and this was a hard setback for the British, as they lost their most competent general in the area.

14- Russia: Kutuzov is informed of the true situation of the Murat Army, which is quite far from the troops stationed in Moscow.

15- Russia: in Moscow Bonaparte is in a desperate situation. This day began to snow, covering the ground a layer of 3 inches of snow, the temperature has dropped yesterday to 0 º C, affecting its 105,000 soldiers, most without more warm clothing than they have found, and hunger threatens them, 550 miles inside a devastated territory, as a result of Kutuzov Burned Earth tactics.

16- Russia: the 90,000 infantrymen and 15,000 horsemen who remain from the Grande Armée begin to leave Moscow, followed by artillery trains, herds of cattle, convoys of chariots loaded with wounded animals, fodder, food and baggage, as well as the loot obtained from looting Russian cities. They are accompanied by hundred of foreign civilians for fear of reprisals they may suffer from the Russians to be their countries allies of the invaders. Napoleon orders to undermine the Kremlin and the Tower of Ivan the Great, among other monuments to proceed to his blast when evacuating the city. The mining is carried out by Russian prisoners, those who refuse are shot. After 3 days, the explosives are ready.

17- Russia: at dawn the Russian army leaves Tarutino to the northeast in five columns, counting the 2nd, 3rd and 4th Army Corps, ten regiments of Cossacks and another of hunters: about 36,000 men. They cross the Nara River and Bennigsen's group hides in a forest near Dmitrovskoe at dusk, while the Denisov Cossacks are placed in their rear with artillery and a regiment of Guards. Napoleon, with a frowning gesture and wrapped in a warm fur coat, leaves Moscow in a big sleigh pulled by 3 horses. Thus begins its long retreat through hostile and icy Russia, for the moment to the southwest, to meet with Murat's troops at Krasnaya Pakhra.

18- Spain, Castillo de Burgos: at 4:00 p.m. the final assault begins, after having breached two gaps. Three columns of Allied soldiers attack with a bayonet, engaging in close hand-to-hand combat with the defenders, who detonate the mines they had placed in the columns of the church of San Roman, burying 300 allies; the rest of the attackers flee in disarray. By then, the French army of Portugal has been reorganized, and General Souham with 40,000 soldiers comes to the aid of the besieged, while the French army of King Joseph Bonaparte leaves Valencia and marches towards the Tagus to conquer Madrid.

Russia: At dawn, Bennigsen's soldiers attack the French left flank, taking Murat's men completely unawares. The Russians cut the French lines and advance northeast to Spas Kuplia, cutting off their withdrawal to Moscow.

At 07:00 the Denisov Cossacks attack the Cuirassiers and Carabineers while they were sleeping in Teterinki, discarding those who are not killed, wounded or imprisoned. Two French regiments are quickly reorganized firing at the Russian Hunters, causing many casualties, killing their general and rejecting two Russian regiments, although the rest continues to advance in good order. Murat establishes an effective defense in Tetrinki, but Bennigsen receives two new reinforcement divisions. In total, 46 Russian battalions are maneuvering towards the village. Another group of Cossacks crosses the Chernisnya flanking the French also by the west, attacking the cavalry of Lateur Mabourg by its rear. Murat is surrounded and orders a retreat towards Moscow, harassed by the Cossacks. The Russian generals ask for more reinforcements to Kutuzov to stop him, but the general refuses, and they abandon the persecution in Spas Kuplia at dawn of the following day. The French escaped thanks to the intervention of the cavalry of Lateur Mabourg and the troops of General Clapared, which allowed them to break the siege by Spas Kuplia, but they left behind 2,500 dead and wounded, 1,000 prisoners, 36 cannons, a lot of gunpowder, ammunition, carriages and a flag. The Russians had 300 dead and 900 wounded. In the camp of the Russian army of Tarutino this triumph raises the morale after the loss of Moscow. Napoleon will fit this defeat with great displeasure Murat has been victim of his overconfidence by underestimating the capabilities of his adversary. South America: a River Plate army under the command of José Rondeau besieges Montevideo for the second time. Artigas enters the Banda Oriental again, but does not participate in the siege.

19- Russia: Until a few days ago, Napoleon was still thinking of stationing himself in the capital and leading an expedition to the Minsk-Smolensk-Vitebsk triangle, west of Moscow, where he could perhaps find fertile land and farms that had not been razed or seized by soldiers Russians But, after the defeat suffered yesterday by Murat near Tarutino, the Russian army is being remade to the southwest of the capital while the French have lost their initial numerical superiority. Finally, the imminent arrival of the cruel Russian winter revokes all plans to continue a campaign to Saint Petersburg next year. Bonaparte has sent a total of three embassies to the Tsar with offers of peace, but he has never replied, evidencing that he intends to continue on the defensive, until the French are weak enough to go on the offensive. The Russian strategy of holding back its natural ally, the "General Winter", has been a success. Spain: Joseph Bonaparte leaves Valencia with a French army, with the intention of recovering Madrid. The Marquis of Wellington cannot face two armies that outnumber him and orders a general retreat to the safety of his forts in Portugal.

20- Russia: in Moscow there remains a French rearguard force of 8,000 soldiers under Marshal Mortier, who must leave the capital once the charges are detonated, on the following day. At dusk the Partisans inform General Docturov that Napoleon and his Guard have reached Fominskoe and are heading to Maloyaroslavets in front of the Grande Armée, of some 105,000 men; Your destination is Kaluga, in search of better weather and supplies. Kutuzov decides to cut them off at Maloyaroslavets, about 120 km southwest of Moscow. Spain: the Anglo-Portuguese divisions of the Tagus retreat to the west, and the garrison of General Hill Madrid leaves the capital after flying works that may be useful to the French, such as some stores of the Retiro and the Royal Porcelain Factory.
Río de la Plata: Gaspar Vigodet, governor of Montevideo, breaks the armistice, but the Argentines of José Rondeau and Lieutenant-Colonel Miguel Stanislaw Soler and Artigas impose a 2nd site to Montevideo.

21- Moscow: Demolitions organized by the French begin, explosions topple some towers of the Kremlin; several cathedrals and palaces are partially demolished and burned down; hundreds of people will be killed or injured, increasing hatred for the French. Meanwhile Kutuzov arrives with his troops to Krasnaya Pakhar, southwest of Moscow, camping there. The Russian artillery of Ivashev covers the three roads that lead to the city of Maloyaroslavets.

22 – Russia: the cavalry of the Army Corps of Doctorov marches towards Aristovo, to attack the enemy's flank. Miloradovich sends troops to explore the Old Road of Kaluga, to find out the position of the French Army Corps commanded by Murat and Ney. Spain: end of the Siege of the Castle of Burgos, Wellington ordered to lift the siege and retreat to Portugal, after having suffered in the frustrated siege about 2,000 casualties; the French lost 600 men. South America: pressured by the Spanish government to move closer to Bogota and before the failure of its campaign of conquest, the viceroy of Nueva Granada Benito Pérez Brito resigns.

23 – Russia: the bulk of the Russian army departs from its Tarutino camp to Maloyaroslavets. Spain France: in Paris, conspiracy of General Malet against Napoleon, the attempted coup d'état fails. Spain: Venta del Pozo combat.

24- Russia: battle of Maloyaroslavets, at dawn the Russian outposts approach Maloyaroslavets, occupying the hills that dominate the city and its bridge over the Luza, blocking the Kaluga road towards which the vanguard of the French column is heading, 15,000 men of the Body of Eugene Beauharnais; two of his battalions enter the city, a regiment of Russian Hunters being evicted in a street shooting. The French withdraw to the other side of the river Luza, to the north of the town; Eugene orders General Delsonne to counterattack with his entire division; Docturov sends two regiments of Hunters as reinforcement, beginning a bloody struggle to dominate the city. The Russian artillery wreaks havoc on the French units advancing towards it; Delsonne himself is mortally wounded, occupying Gillermino his place. The troops of Gillermino, superior in number to the Russians, make them retreat and take over Maloyaroslavets, followed by the division of Brussier. The French do not stop at the village, they continue advancing south, to attack the Russian positions half a kilometer from the city. These are reinforced by the arrival of the rest of the Docturov Corps, with its 20,000 soldiers. The Russian infantry regiments of Libavsky and Sophiysky go out to meet the French supported by their artillery; Gillermino retreats to Maloyaroslavets, where bloody street fighting again, with discharges of rifle and bayonet charges; several fires erupt in the city. At dawn the first troops of the French Army Corps of Davout and the Imperial Guard arrive in the area, adding to the clashes, which intensify with the arrival of the 7th Russian Corps of General Raevsky. The bulk of the Russian army of Kutuzov has advanced up to 5 km south of the city. At 15:00 hours, the Russians of Docturov and Raevsky have expelled the French from Maloyaroslavets, but then Napoleon appears in the area, and orders Marshal Davout that two of his divisions join Eugene's troops and assault another time the villa; one part will attack by a bridge that the French engineers build in the Luza and another by the bridge of the village. In a quick assault the French conquer Maloyaroslavets. Then are came the bulk of the Russian army, adding more than 90,000 soldiers to the fight, located in the hills on both sides of the road to Kaluga. Kutuzov orders several units to expel the invaders from Maloyaroslavets, initiating another bloody street fight. Napoleon perceives that almost all the Russian army is present, while only 63,000 French have arrived; the rest is still on the way. At night the fighting ceases. Maloyaroslavets is burning with its streets full of corpses. The French have suffered 5,000 casualties, the Russians about 6,000. Bonaparte meets with his staff in a house in the village of Gorodina, and after analyzing the situation, concludes that Kutuzov occupies the best positions and has a larger number of soldiers whose morale is high and well equipped. Bonaparte is at a great disadvantage and knows that tomorrow the decisive battle will be fought.

25- Russia: at dawn Napoleon plans to break the Russian lines and goes to Maloyaroslavets to inspect the front. But Platov's Cossacks, who crossed the Luza River at night, charge by surprise against the rearguard of the Poles of Poniatowsky, disbanding it. The Russians were about to capture Bonaparte himself, who is in the company of Marshal Berthier, the General Rapp and some officers, protected by only 25 Guard soldiers. The Cossacks attack them, when two squadrons of cavalry come to their aid. The Russians decide to attack the French camp, steal several horses and cannons and then disappear into a forest. After inspecting the excellent Russian positions and the razed Maloyaroslavets, Napoleon returns to Gorodina and decides to abandon his plan to retreat south and do it to the west, to Viazma. He is so shocked by the brutal Cossack attack that he orders Dr. Juvanne to prepare a small bottle of poison that he will always wear around his neck, so that he will not be captured alive. Spain: Battle of Villa

Muriel. United States: the United States ship United States, commanded by Captain Stephen Decatur, sighted off the coast of Madeira the British Macedonian ship, captured it and took it to Connecticut.

The Battle of Maloyaroslavets has been a great victory for Kutuzov, forcing the French to retreat into areas without supplies, to be razed in the summer, and in colder latitudes.

26- Caucasus: victory of the Russians of Pyotr Kotlyarevsky at the Battle of Aslanduz on the Persians of Abbas Mirza; Britain's Sir Gore Ouseley is in charge of mediating between Persians and Russians.
Mexico: Jose Maria Morelos occupies the city of Orizaba after expelling the small royalist garrison that defended it.

27- South America: Chilean dictator José Miguel Carrera promulgated a Provisional Constitutional Regulation, prepared with the collaboration of the American consul, which established a Governmental Superior Board of three members and a Senate of seven members with legislative power. Theoretically, the text recognized the sovereignty of King Ferdinand VII, but his fifth article stated that no decree, order or order emanating from any authority or courts outside the territory of Chile will have any effect; and those who try to give them value will be punished as inmates of the State. This in practice established the independence of Chile.

28- Russia: the Cossacks of Ataman Platov, the most versatile unit of the Russian army, harasses the withdrawal of the Grande Armée to Viazma, assaulting the invaders as they pass through Mozaisk and Gzhastsk. Spain: Combat of Tordesillas. North America: Morelos leaves Tehuacán, wins in Escamela and the royalists leave Ixtaczoquitlán, soon after, with 10,000 men, Morelos conquers Orizaba, in Veracruz.

29- Russia continues at war with Persia, but that does not affect her effort against the French; in Persian territory, this afternoon, 2,000 Russians with six cannons massacred a Persian army of 30,000 soldiers in Aslanduz.

30 - Spain: Spain: Combat of Puente Largo. South America: the troops of Lieutenant General Toribio Montes, appointed president of the Audience of Quito, conquer Popayan for Spain and after defeating the patriots in Mocha they enter Quito, where Montes exerts a harsh repression, defeating definitively the Quito patriots.

31- Russia: battle of the Kolotsky monastery: Platov concentrates his 20 regiments and directs a charge against the left flank of the rear of the French column, annihilating more than two battalions, taking 20 cannons, two flags and a large number of carriages with their baggage. The fear of the French for the incursions of the Cossacks increases; his morale drops as much as the temperatures, which are already around -4º C. Second Combat of Polotsk: Wittgenstein makes the French flee. In Spain: after the departure of the English to Alba de Tormes, the governor of Madrid, Don Carlos of Spain, is left without enough troops to defend the capital. Mexico: on his way to Tehuacán, Morelos is surprised in Acultzingo by Colonel Aquila and loses many men and all the artillery recently captured.

NOVEMBER-1812

1- Russia: combat of Zaïmitché. Rio de la Plata: the governor of Montevideo, Gaspar Vigodet, tries to break the siege and makes an exit with his army, but is defeated in the battle of Miguelete.

2- Spain: King Joseph Bonaparte enters Madrid again, without encountering any opposition.

3- Russia: battles of Viazma and Fedorovskoe. Napoleon with his Imperial Guard, marching in the vanguard of the French column, arrives at Semlevo after having crossed Viazma; After him marched the 3rd Army Corps of Marshal Ney, who has just left the city, while the 4th and 5th Corps of Eugene and Poniatowsky are approaching, about 7 km; In the rear of the column the 1st Corps of Marshal Davout closes, in Fedorovskoe, 17 km. Bonaparte is informed that the Corps of Saint-Cyr and Oudinot, who march in another column protecting their right flank, west of the Dvina River, are attacked by General Wittgenstein's troops. For their part, the Platov Cossacks chase the Davout troops close to Federovskoe, attacking them throughout the march. The vanguard of the Russian army, with the 2nd and 4th Corps under the Milordarovich, supported by the 2nd and 4th Corps of cavalry and five regiments of Cossacks, march to Viazma, reaching Spasskoe while the bulk of Kutozov's army is in Dubrova, 26 km from Viazma. Kutozov plans to bag the troops of Davout, Eugene and Poniatowsky. Send Milordarovich and two divisions of Cuirassiers of Uvarov to cut them off and interrupt communications with Napoleon on the road to Smolensk, to the west, at the same time the Platov Cossacks attack the French by their rear, to the east; while, Kutozov advances towards Viazma from Byokovo to intercept any help sent by Bonaparte.

At 08:00 hours, Milordarovich leaves Spasskoe and cuts the Smolensk road where the 4th and 5th Corps of Eugene and Poniatowsky will arrive, deploying their 2nd and 4th Corps before Viazma, while their cavalry harasses them seconded by artillery fire by the flanks. The Platov Cossacks attack the 1st Corps of Davout, in Fedorovskoe, surrounding all the troops of Eugene, Poniatowsky and Davout. Marshals Eugene and Poniatowsky are in a desperate situation, both isolated from the column and surrounded. They try to join forces with Davout to organize a better defense; but the artillery and cavalry of Milordarovich press them by the flanks forcing them to desist; then the attack of the Russian infantry begins. The French suffer many casualties. Eugene and Poniatowsky note that some units of Milordarovich maneuver towards Viazma, where most of the carriages and supplies of the Grande Armée are, then occupy the hills near the city to place their artillery, which with their fire stops the Russian maneuver. Meanwhile, the men of Davout manage to leave Fedorovskoe and advance, regrouping to the east of Viazma about 37,000 French soldiers. The forces of Milordarovich and Platov are concentrated around him receiving continuous reinforcements, until reaching about 25,000 Russian soldiers. At 14:00 hours, the Russians attack, crushing the French formations and pushing them into the interior of Viazma, where they improvise defenses.

At 16:00 Milordarovich orders the Platov Cossacks, aided by Partisans of Seslavin, to lead the assault on Viazma, followed by other regiments of Russian infantry.

Towards 02:00 hours of the morning of the following day the combats finish, being the city in flames. The French withdraw from the city at night to Dorogobuzh, but they have suffered 6,000 casualties and another 2,500 have been captured. The Russians enter Viazma, releasing 300 of their imprisoned officers locked in a church about to collapse. The Russian casualties are unknown. The 90,000 soldiers left to the Grande Armée are demoralized, indiscipline spreads, and casualties increase due to cold, temperatures have dropped to - 6º C. Since leaving Moscow, the French army has lost some 15,000 men; the fighting spirit of his troops has diminished, becoming frightened when he sees the Cossacks or Partisans marauding; they watch them constantly, riding near their columns or stalking them among the trees, killing deserters and laggards, the invading soldiers are held together to have a chance to stay alive. Napoleon tries to inspire his troops confidence in their maneuvers to return to the homeland; He still believes that Tsar Alexander I will parley with him. The French soldiers walk under the snow in long columns towards Smolensk.

5- United States: presidential election, after a hard-fought election campaign, President James Madison gets re-elected, defeats DeWitt Clinton.

7- Russia: the Partisans of Davidov, Seslavin and Figner, advance towards the west by the south of the road of Smolensko, arriving at Elnya, while the brigade of General Augerau, of about 2,500 men, advances towards Liakovo. Spain: Joseph Bonaparte leaves Madrid at the command of his troops in pursuit of the Anglo-Portuguese, after leaving a garrison in the capital.

The French occupy part of Spain with a powerful army of 230,000 soldiers: Soult has 56,000 in Andalusia, Suchet 60,000 in Aragon and Catalonia, Claussel 52,000 in the south Castile, Dorsenne 48,000 in the Basque and northern Castile; King José Bonaparte has another 12,000 men in Madrid. For its part, the Marquis of Wellington has only about 55,000 soldiers. However, Napoleon, his brother Joseph and his generals disagree about the occupation of Spain: the first wants to annex to France the territory north of the Ebro, emulating the Hispanic Mark of Charlemagne, the second intends to reign throughout the country, but his generals do not respect his authority, each one tending to exploit and defend the region he occupies, showing reluctance to collaborate with others. Due to this lack of coordination, the French do not gather their troops and carry out an offensive against the allies, despite outnumbering them; Wellington knows these disagreements and will take advantage of them in the future. In addition, the invaders must guard themselves of some 50,000 soldiers and militiamen distributed by the Peninsula, supported by the guerrilla parties, with at least another 30,000 men.

8- Combat of Liakovo: When the Russians of Denisov join the Partisans, they decide to attack the French unit that occupies the town, distanced from the rest of the Grande Armée. This morning, some 1,500 Russian Partisans commanded by Denisov attack the Augerau brigade in Liakovo, and although it is hard-fought, the attackers kill many of them by catching them by surprise, and manage to isolate them completely from the rest of the French army; the defenders finally surrender. The Russians made about 400 casualties and captured more than 2,000 soldiers and about 60 officers.

9 – Russia: combats on the Smolensk Road. Napoleon, accompanied by his Imperial Guard, enters Smolensk while the rear of the Grande Armée is harshly attacked by the Cossacks and Partisans. During the next four days the soldiers who manage to get to the city will be able to rest while waiting for the stragglers to regroup. Bonaparte now has about 60,000 soldiers able to fight another 15,000 are in terrible condition because of the cold, which has claimed the lives of thousands of men. The 5th and 8th Bodies of Poniatowsky and Junot have only 800 soldiers each; and the 4th of Eugene has fewer men still. Among all the cavalry corps, including the reserve corps, there are about 5,000 horsemen. The 1st and 3rd Bodies of Davout and Ney are the most numerous, but the morale of their troops has declined due to the defeats suffered. The Imperial Guard has had few losses and its morale is still high, although it has also suffered the rigors of weather. In addition, the French army is accompanied by artillery trains, food carts and caravans of hundreds of Muscovite civilians, and thousands of wounded or sick soldiers. In Smolensk the temperature is lower than that suffered by those who come on the road, about -12 º C, and continues to descend daily. Napoleon finds few supplies in the city, so the cold will add to the hunger, because although there is still sustenance for a few days, the last Russian attacks have deprived them of wagons and cattle. The fearsome "General Winter", the ancient natural ally of Russia, looms over the Grande Armée during its painful retreat to Smolensk: the temperatures drop today to -11º C, giving continuous blizzards of very thick snow. Among the soldiers there is a shortage of warm clothes and shoes; some line their boots in rags of uniforms and cloaks, snatched from dead comrades or enemies, and even wear horse skin.

10- Russia: Battle of the Vop River: The 4th French Army Corps, commanded by Eugene de Beauharnais, is sent by Napoleon to evacuate the garrison of Vitebsk, harassed by the Russians. The Cossacks of Ataman Platov observe the maneuver of this column and go against it after seeing it depart from Dorogobuzh, with the intention of attacking it. This morning the French arrive at the river Vop, but they doubt where to cross it when finding their only bridge destroyed. Precisely then, a group of Platov's Cossacks begins to shoot them, charging against them, while another group crosses the river and attacks them from the other shore. Eugene fears being surrounded and desperately orders the retreat, fording the river disorderly. United Kingdom general election, the Tory Party is victorious, under Robert Jenkinson, 2nd Earl of Liverpool.

11- Russia: Solovieva combats: General Milordarovich's troops, at the forefront of the Russian army, expelled the French in Dorogobuzh on November 7, liberating the city, but later turned south to meet with the bulk of their army, sending the General Yurkovsky with a detachment of soldiers, supported by the Cossacks of Karpov, to harass the retreat of Marshal Ney's 3rd Corps on the road to Smolensk. The Russians arrive at the Solovieva crossing, attacking Ney's column, capturing about 1,000 prisoners and 21 cannons before retreating.

12- Russia: during the morning and afternoon of this day, the Cossack riders and the Russian Partisans, very accustomed to their harsh climate and well equipped against the cold, harass the forces of the rear of the Grande Armée while retreating on the road to Smolensk, causing them about 13,000 casualties, in addition to seizing quantities of wagons, supplies, equipment and weapons. The Cossacks fiercely attack the French rearguard, with such ferocity that the demoralized soldiers disperse in panic. The Russians cause about 2,000 casualties, capture another 4,500 and seize 64 of their 87 cannons. Eugene manages to escape, but the 4th Army Corps has disappeared as a fighting force. North America: the Yankee filibuster Augustus W. Magee, who had left his army to serve Mexico with the rank of colonel, left Natchitoches, Louisiana, in early August at the head of an expedition of 130 men called the Republican Army of the North, crossed the Sabine River where he was joined by José Bernardo Maximilian Gutierrez de Lara, leader of the revolution in Nuevo Santander, entered Nacogdoches, Texas, with whose authorities he had conspired, and with an army expanded to 300 he briefly occupied the Most Holy Trinity from Salcedo in mid-September and the La Bahía prison, trying to separate Texas from Spain, Governor Salcedo immediately besieges La Bahía this morning, where Magee will be ill, perhaps malaria or poisoned.

13- Russia: Bonaparte decides to leave Smolensk to resume the withdrawal to the west and leave Russia before the weather conditions worsen. The Emperor plans to raise another new and larger army, with the intention of returning to invade the Tsar's domain next year; pretense considered unrealizable by its staff officers. The French army will leave Smolensk in five groups, which will depart on different days towards Krasnoe; this morning the Corps of Poniatowsky and Junot come out in the vanguard. Kutozov is informed that Napoleon leaves Smolensk in columns, and plans to attack them independently and sporadically, first ordering General Milordarovich to cut the road between Smolensko and Krasniy, where the French are heading. The Cossack regiments of Denisov and the Partisans of Davidov will also attend the area. The troops of Milordarovich take positions near Krasnoe, so that they can beat the way by which the French will come placing artillery. In Pzahvka, his men attack the stragglers of the Imperial Guard, taking 2,000 prisoners and taking 11 cannons.

14- Russia: the evacuation of Smolensk continues; this morning Napoleon and his Imperial Guard leave. Combats of Klementino and Alexevo: the Cossacks of Denisov find in the afternoon a convoy of French wagons, transporting food and fodder, near the towns of Klemiatino and Alexevo. The Cossacks assault the convoy, causing the French 1,500 casualties and taking 1,300 prisoners, 400 carriages full of supplies, 1,000 draft horses and 200 cattle. The third combat of Polotsk is fought.

15- Russia: evacuation of Smolensk, departure of the Corps of Eugene. Combats on the Road to Krasnoe: the forces of General Borozdin and the Cossacks of Denisov attack the French columns at various points, managing to separate small groups of soldiers who are then captured or killed, which may mean the same thing; it is rumored that the Cossacks flay their captives. The Partisans of Davidov, Seslavin and Figner make several ambushes that cause more casualties to the French near Orsha. Continually harassed and watched, the demoralized French lose all capacity for tactical initiative; the soldiers remain united only to leave Russia alive, but they are on the verge of insubordination, and more and more people risk desertion. The losses by cold begin to cause havoc between them, the temperature has descended abruptly to -26º C. 15- Battle of Krasnoe or Krasniy: Kutozov decides to ambush the retreat of the columns of the Grande Armée in Krasnoe, and sends four Army Corps camping some 4 km to the southeast, while two other Corps under Milordarovich are positioned to the northeast, in the road of Smolensk, where the French will come, who must pass without delay to the west of Krasnoe to escape Russia. Kutuzov deploys a wall of fire south of Krasnoe. Milordarovich will attack the French vanguard in a limited way with the 2nd and 7th Bodies, allowing them to pass within reach of the rifles and cannons of the 5th, 6th, and 8th Bodies of Tormasov, deployed to the south with a division of Cuirassiers; to then attack them from the rear with the support of Golitsyn, with the 3rd Russian Corps and another division of Cuirassiers. Milordarovich attacks the 4th Corps of Eugene, while the Poniatowsky Corps and the Imperial Guard troops, escorting Napoleon, pass their flanks and enter Krasnoe; where the Young Guard must defend against the attack of several units of Tormasov and Golitsyn, while the men of Eugene are flanked and flee in flight to a forest, to later regroup in Krasnoe.

16- Russia: evacuation of Smolensk, the Davout Corps leaves the city. Bonaparte goes out on the road to the west of Krasnoe with the Imperial Guard while the 5th Corps of Poniatowsky is harassed from the south by Tormasov's vanguards. Meanwhile, Davout's 1st Corps arrives in Krasnoe, in the center of the retreating column. Milordarovich allows him to pass and then attack him from the rear; the French flee into the woods or seek refuge in Krasnoe, abandoning artillery, carriages, even some soldiers throw their weapons. Davout tries to organize the resistance in the town, trying to regroup his demoralized troops, who are shot and grained by the Russians from the south; retiring with such haste by the panic, that they suffer very few casualties. The marshal manages to unite them and forms a solid line to the southeast of the town that contains the advance of the Russians of Tormasov. Napoleon orders several units of the Imperial Guard to go back in support of the 1st Corps. The 16,000 soldiers of the Guard carry out several charges of cavalry against the 35,000 Russians, causing them to retreat. In Minsk there is an intense combat.

17 – Russia: evacuation of Smolensk, the Ney Corps is the last to leave the city and its forts in flames. In the afternoon, the French leave Krasnoe in the west when the Ney Corps arrives, with its soldiers and a few thousand civilians. Napoleon concludes that he cannot do anything for him and his men, and orders to resume the march, going to Dubrovno; the Russians send a division of Cuirassiers west of Krasnoe to ensure their departure. Ney tries to break through Krasnoe by force, but the abundant artillery of Milordarovich stops his attack. The Russians go to the counterattack, and the 3rd French Corps retires towards the north, towards the town of Syrokorenie, but the Russian cavalry pursues it carrying out successive charges, causing an authentic massacre. Several thousand French soldiers surrender, but Ney and another 3,000 manage to reach the Dnieper. Marshal Ney will cross the frozen Dnieper to go to Orsha and return again with Napoleon, drowned hundreds of soldiers and civilians who accompanied him as the ice cracked. In total, they would lose their lives, about 13,000 French would be captured or disappeared in Krasnoe and its surroundings; the Russian casualties are unknown. Spain: combat of San Muñoz.

18- Spain: Wellington arrives in Ciudad Rodrigo near the Portuguese border; his troops have very low morale spreading indiscipline, being on the verge of insubordination. To cover his withdrawal, Wellington asks the governor of Alba de Tormes, José Miranda Cabezón, to defend the local castle whenever possible, to attract the French who persecute his army.

19- Russia: in the city of Orsha, Napoleon regroups and reorganizes his troops. The Grande Armée has about 50,000 soldiers able to fight, most of them are French; another 10,000 accompany them but they barely have the strength to walk; most of them are Italians, Germans, Poles and Dutch, who march without any motivation other than surviving the cold. They are followed by another 40,000 stragglers, as artillerymen without cannons or furriers, and civilian refugees. The temperature has risen to -14 ° C, but continued exposure to the cold is causing havoc, because the French and their allies do not have adequate clothing. And to this is added the absolute lack of food; there are no reserves of victuals, nor cattle to be sacrificed. During the last week the expedition has lost several thousand men as a result of the cold and precarious feeding, apart from the Russian attacks. The majority of the survivors are the troops of the Imperial Guard, among which the Old Guard stands out, and the men of the 1st Corps of Davout. The 3rd, 4th, 5th and 8th Bodies of Ney, Eugene, Poniatowsky and Junot have practically disappeared because they have less than a thousand soldiers each in a position to fight, totaling some 20,000 men altogether. To this army they are united in Botr the 2nd and 6th Corps of Oudinot and Saint Cyr who retire from Polotsk, and the 9th of Victor, stationed in areas of northwest Russia since the beginning of the campaign; it is these units that can strengthen the Grande Armée because they are in better conditions. The other two Corps, the 10th MacDonald and the Austrian Schwarzenberg march further northwest and southeast protecting the flanks.

20 – Russia: Bonaparte leaves Orsha abandoning almost all the artillery, except 250 pieces, and many wagons with equipment, to try to lighten the march and accelerate the exit of Russia. All material that is not declared essential is destroyed. United States: American militiamen captured a British outpost near Lacolle, in Quebec. However, during the night another group of militiamen attacked them, confusing them with the British, and the real British took advantage of the confusion to recover the fort and put the Americans to flight.

21- Russia: hundreds of famished men die of cold, leaving their corpses frozen in the gutters of the roads. Their companions search them for food and snatch their warm clothes and boots, but no one buries them. Neither the sick injured or dying receive assistance. The draft horses begin to be sacrificed to eat their meat. The French army is heading towards the Beresina River, the last major obstacle on its way to Vilnius and the Niemen River, on the border with Prussia, supposedly salvation. The Russian Cossacks and Partisans harass him from the south continually, trying to break their formations to isolate small groups or seize carriages, in an incessant maneuver of attrition; but his attacks cannot disperse Napoleon's Old Guard.

22- Russia: two days after departing from Orsha, the French vanguard arrives near Studenka, spotting ice sheets floating on the Beresina, a large river, about 400 meters wide. Napoleon is desolate because he expected to find the river frozen, with a thick layer of ice that would allow him to cross it. Now he must build a bridge, the one that existed has been demolished by the Russians. Meanwhile, Chichagov surrounds the Austrian Schwarzenberg Corps of 30,000 soldiers, which Napoleon left to the southwest while advancing through Russia in summer, and arrives in Borisov. After defeating the unit of Poles, it captures 2,000 prisoners. Chichagov deploys his men to the shore of the Beresina, while Wittgenstein advances from the north and Kutuzov from the east. Napoleon orders Oudinot and Victor to mobilize their Army Corps and evict Chicagov from the east bank of the Beresina and drive Wittgenstein away from Studenka, containing him in Borisov, while Bonaparte himself would cross the river with the remains of his expedition to flee from Kutuzov.

23- Russia: Bonaparte sends a unit of Poles to occupy Borisov, about 23 miles to the south by the river Beresina, to contain the Russians allowing their troops from Orsha to reach Beresina, while the bridges are being built. Kutuzov plans to make one last great attack against the Grande Armée in the Beresina, cutting them off and closing them. While heading with 80,000 soldiers of the 3rd Russian Army to the south, accompanying the French withdrawal, Admiral Chichagov with 34,000 men marches towards Borisov, on the west bank of the river, and the 30,000 Wittgenstein soldiers are positioned to the north.

24 – Russia: the 2nd Corps of Oudinot arrives at Loshnistsy, finding a Russian outpost that alerts Chichagov; while the French enter Borisov, protecting the southern flank of the French withdrawal. The Russians retired to 25 km to the southwest, leaving two battalions of infantry and three regiments of Cossacks near Borisov. On the same day, about 400 French Sappers under the supervision of Murat and Mortier, intend to build three bridges to cross the river from Studenka, where the width of the river is 90 to 150 meters. Spain: combat of Alba de Tormes, the Allied army under the command of Wellington retires to Portugal from Burgos, passing through Torquemada, Cordobilla, Cabezón de Campos, Duero Bridge; Tudela until arriving in Salamanca, pursued by the French outposts of the Portuguese Army commanded by Souham. The Anglo-Portuguese destroy the bridges to delay the French, engaging in sporadic fighting. The demoralized allies enter Portugal, camping north of the impregnable Fortified Line of Torres Vedras, deploying from Lamego to the Sierras de Baños and Béjar, in Salamanca. Meanwhile, an avalanche of French is launched against the walls and parapets of Alba de Tormes. The people of Salamanca contain the French defending the castle and making exits until the early hours of today, when the governor orders to evacuate the city, because it is in ruins because of enemy artillery fire. They remain in the city, to protect the retreat, Lieutenant Nicolas Solar, with 20 soldiers, in addition to 33 wounded or sick; and 112 French prisoners.

25- Russia: the French begin construction to build three bridges, dismantling several Studenka houses. That afternoon begins a snow storm that makes the work difficult, work day and night. The temperatures rise progressively, causing desperation to the soldiers who wait impatient to cross to the other side, while the Russians of Kutuzov approach by the east and those of Wittgenstein by the north. At 17:00 hours the General of Engineers Jean Baptiste Eblé arrives in Studenka, who will take charge of the works, speeding them up. He brings with him forges, coal, nails and other tools rescued from the materials that Bonaparte ordered destroyed in Orsha. Decides to build two bridges instead of the three planned ones; one will be more solid, to bear the weight of artillery and carriages; both will be about 5 meters wide. The first bridge, for the infantry, ends at dusk. Mexico: Jose Maria Morelos managed to occupy the city of Oaxaca, the first important city that fell into his power.

26- Russia: that morning at 01:00, the French of the 2nd Corps of Oudinot begin to cross the river with the division of Legrand in front. They are followed by Napoleon and 11,000 soldiers of his Young Guard; Bonaparte will cross again to the eastern bank of the Beresina to direct the retreat. Towards 04:00 hours, the Engineers finish the heaviest bridge; the artillery and the transport cars begin to cross it in good order, but the bridge is precarious and collapses twice during this early morning, stopping the crossing of cannons and carriages to be repaired.

27- Russia: some cars with materials and tools arrive from Orsha, to help in the construction of the bridges over the Beresina. The Cossacks of Platov and Ermolov, and the Partisans of Seslavin, in the vanguard of the 3rd Russian Army, arrive at Borisov from the southeast, while Wittgenstein arrives in the northeast, engaging in a very hard battle with the troops of Oudinot and Victor defending the town. The division of Partunot, of the 9º Corps of Victor, resists in principle, but ends up surrendering before the numerical superiority of the Russians; about 4,000 French are captured and another 2,000 die in combat. After taking Borisov, Wittengstein turns north and continues advancing to Studenka along the eastern bank of the Beresina, in coordination with Chichagov's troops, which move north along the western bank, with 72,000 Russians hovering over the French; the vanguard of the 3rd Kutuzov Army that are approaching. Victor's troops retreat to Studenka and Oudinot's troops follow him, but preparing to cross to the west bank by the bridges. On the eastern bank, the troops of the 1st and 9th Corps of Davout and Victor and the Old Guard form a solid defensive line southeast of Studenka, to cover those who retreat over the bridges. At 4:00 pm. the main bridge, through which the artillery and the wagons cross, collapses again, the withdrawal is interrupted until the sappers finish their repair, working for hours in appalling conditions due to the growing cold; Many workers lose their lives in the task. South America: Battle of Ibarra, decisive defeat of the troops of Quito; the Spanish enter the city of Ibarra and shoot more than 70 people.

28- Russia: the troops of Chichagov, Ermolov and the Platov Cossacks, attack the 600 survivors of the 3rd Corps of Ney by the south of the west bank, and the soldiers of the 2nd of Oudinot who have just arrived at this shore, in total 12,000 men, who manage to stop the Russian attacks. Meanwhile, on the eastern bank, Wittengstein emplace his artillery and bombard the French line southeast of Studenka, while his infantry march to the bridges. In the face of the coordinated Russian attack on the two shores, and the closeness of Kutuzov's 3rd Army, the organization of the French soldiers collapses completely in panic. Waves of soldiers leave their positions and camps to throw themselves into the bridges to escape, followed by a crowd of civilians, without attending any discipline beyond their individual desire to survive. Napoleon, contemplating the growing hysteria, leaves the eastern shore of the Beresina by one of the bridges, at around 2:00 p.m. The Old Guard opens the way, while they retire in disorder next to the 1st and 4th Bodies of Davout and Eugene, and many stragglers who enter the bridges. In the chaos, thousands of soldiers and refugees die hit or trampled by others, crushed by cars or animals, drowned or frozen in the cold waters, or hit by sporadic Russian gunfire. One of the bridges collapses due to the great weight of floats, cannons, horses and people, so the crowd concentrates on the entrance of the other, making evacuation difficult, the column advances only a few steps every hour, between horrible deafening scenes explosions, screams of men, cries of women, and cries of children. By 4:00 pm, only the 9th Corps of Victor remains on the western bank, southeast of Studenka; all other units are already west of the Beresina. Through the bridges a crowd continues fleeing to the west, abandoning their carriages in the quagmire of access to the pontoons, which makes access difficult. Victor's soldiers contain the Wittgenstein Russians until nightfall, and then retire; At 9:00 p.m. they arrive at the western shore, while the pathetic crowd continues to overflow the bridges until late at night. On the western bank the troops of Oudinot, Ney and the Guard have been able to contain the Russians of Chichagov until the fighting ceases, at around 11:00 p.m. By then, the Russians who harass them are very high morale, confident in their greater number and well protected against the cold, but they lack food: due to their own tactic of Burned Earth, the surrounding areas are depleted. They register all the prisoners and cars of the invaders they capture; but the French are worse off: dejected, hungry and suffering up to -25º C during the day, and even some - 29º C at night.

 29- Russia: all the Army Corps and organized French or allied formations have already crossed to the western shore of the Beresina. From the moment of its opening, there were sentinels at the entrance of each bridge to prevent anyone unarmed from crossing them; in such a way that the majority of French who still remain on the eastern bank are civilians and soldiers wounded, sick or dying, stragglers from their units or lost, many unarmed, without any military direction. At 09:00 in the morning, Eblé orders to burn the only bridge left standing, to prevent the Russians of Wittgenstein and Milordarovich from pursuing the withdrawal of the French army to the west, leaving the hundreds of people who are crossing them to die and abandoning to their lot the thousands who were on the east bank of the river, while on the west bank, the Cossacks of Chichagov charge once more against the French rear, now under Victor, being rejected. Some 28,000 French soldiers with 200 guns have managed to cross the Beresina, followed by 30,000 auxiliary soldiers and civilian refugees; the first left behind 32,000 casualties, and the stragglers suffered another 10,000; all the Sappers who erected the bridges died. In the fighting, the Russians had 20,000 casualties.

The crossing of the Berezina is considered a success for Napoleon, because it could have been annihilated by the numerical superiority of the Kutuzov troops.

DECEMBER-1812

1- Mexico: Morelos, at the head of 5,000 men, defeats the 600 royalists of Lieutenant General Antonio Gonzalez de Saravia and Mollinedo in Oaxaca, takes the city and shoots Gonzalez, General José María de Régules Villasante and other high-ranking officers.

2- United States: the political situation of the different States that were emerging in New Granada and other regions of South America contrasted with that of the United States, where the federalists also maintained their discrepancies with the Democratic Republicans, but, even in time of war, nothing altered the electoral process for the election of the new president. The Democratic Republicans presented Madison for re-election and, as Vice President Clinton had died, they replaced him with Elbridge Gerry of Massachusetts. It was no coincidence that the vice presidential candidate was from New England, because it was the most critical region with Madison and the war against Great Britain. The federalists presented as a candidate for president the mayor of New York, Dewitt Clinton, who was the candidate for president proposed by the Republican Democrats opposed to the war. As a candidate for vice president they chose Charles Pared Ingersoll of Pennsylvania. The result was that Madison was re-elected as president, but federalists nearly doubled the number of their representatives in Congress, although the majority remained a Republican Democrat.

3- South America: in New Granada, the tensions between centralists and federalists led to a civil war. The first confrontation took place this day in Ventaquemada, and the federalists were the winners. Antonio Nariño, the president of the State of Cundinamarca and leader of the centralists, offered to surrender with certain conditions, but the federalists demanded an unconditional surrender and the war continued.

4 - Russia: Molodzezno combat. Russian troops, suffering from hunger, rush to looting the peasants and villages. Spain: restructuring of the Spanish Army. By a decree of the Council of Regency of Cadiz, the Hispanic army is divided into 4 main groups: General Copóns, in Catalonia, with 16,000 soldiers, Elío, in Murcia, with 20,000, the Duque del Parque, in

Andalusia, with 12,000 Sicilian soldiers, and the reserve of 12,000 soldiers who garrison Cadiz, commanded by O'Donell. General Castaños unifies in Castile the guerrilla parties of Porlier, Jáurigui, Bárcenas and Mendizábal. Arthur Wellesley, Marquis of Wellington, is named Generalissimo of all Hispanic armies, against the wishes of Spanish generals.

5- Napoleon admits sadly: "I no longer have an army ... For days I have marched in the midst of a flock of disorganized men who roam the fields just in search of food ..." That's why he decides to go ahead, to get Quick to Paris, minimize his defeat and raise a new Grande Armée with which to carry out another campaign and subdue Tsar Alexander I. Many generals ask him to stay, because his absence will cause an absolute demoralization and will disband what is left of his troops; but Napoleon leaves, assuming that his army is near Prussia and that his generals will be able to begin the reorganization there, without needing his presence. In this way he concludes his intervention in the dramatic Russian invasion. Your last order is for the units to burn all their flags. After crossing the Berezina, Kutozov allows the withdrawal of Napoleon's contingent to Vilna, but sends the troops of Chicagov and Wittgenstein against the French on the northern flank and to Milordarovich against the Austrians on the southern flank. The Russian soldiers, although well equipped against the cold, are tired, and especially hungry to the point of starvation, because they lack any logistics. The Platov Cossacks regularly assault the French column in search of some food, and steal what they can from the poor peasants. Temperatures continued to drop to -30 º C on December 1, and since then some nights can reach up to -37 º C. Thousands of French, sheltered in rags and without any protection for the face, suffer evils like the loss of fingers, extremities, lips, nose and eyes, walking through the snow until they die frozen. The hunger is such that after finishing sacrificing most of the horses, some soldiers eat insects or come to stew meat from their deceased companions after snatching the clothes they can use. Except for the Imperial Guard, the rest of the French units are broken, mixed and totally disorganized. The Grande Armée has lost all its military value, degenerated into a column of famished and cold people who care for their survival, fighting each other for what little they have, and defending themselves from the Cossacks' attacks if they are in groups, or fleeing if they are few.

6- Russia: on his way through Lithuania Napoleon was informed of the coup attempt that had taken place in Paris. Concerned about this news, he summoned a great council of war in Smorghoni, instructed Murat to take command and marched in a sledge ready to arrive in Paris as soon as possible.

7- Russia: the French vanguard arrives in Vilna: thousands of them no longer have the strength to continue, dying of hunger or freezing at the gates of the city, sitting on the porches or lying in the streets. Ironically, the inhabitants will bury them in the trenches that the invaders dug in the summer to protect the garrison.

8- Russia: while Bonaparte travels to Warsaw escorted by his Guard, Marshal Ney manages to group a few hundred soldiers willing to fight, repelling some attacks from the Cossacks, hoping to reach the Neman soon and escape from Russia; Ney will be the commander-in-chief of what remains of the Grande Armée. North America: in the so-called "year of earthquakes" in Alta California, an earthquake destroys the mission of San Juan Capistrano, killing 29 people and topples the bell tower of the church of San Gabriel.

Between November 29 and December 4, about 16,000 French people die, mostly from starvation, illness, medical neglect and freeze damage. Another 4,000 more soldiers and some 16,000 auxiliaries and civilians will fall for the same causes until December 9; by then the daytime temperature reaches -34º C.

9 - Combat in Vilna; the French abandon all their artillery.

10- Russia: Platov's Cossacks enter Vilna in pursuit of the French withdrawal. General Luason tried to organize the defense of the capital of Lithuania, but of his 15,000 soldiers, no less than 9,000 died of illness and cold, the others join the 10,000 Ney soldiers in their withdrawal to Prussia.

11- United States: After the Mexican independence revolt was put down in Texas, one of its supporters, Bernardo Gutierrez de Lara, went to the United States in search of support and appeared before the House of Representatives, but barely obtained the guarantee that the States United would not interfere in their projects.

13- Tonight French troops arrive in Kovno, where they can eat some food and rest. Interestingly, the local people believed that Napoleon had achieved a great victory in Berezina, and completely ignored the defeat of the Grande Armée in Russia.

14- Russia: the 10,000 French soldiers and allied survivors of the 420,000 who invaded Tsar Alexander's dominions seven months ago, cross again in the opposite direction the Niemen River, the border between Russia and Prussia, still persecuted by the indefatigable Cossacks of Platov; Some Russians have crossed to the west bank of the river and open fire on isolated groups. In Russia, Napoleon has lost more than 400,000 soldiers, all his artillery, some 580 pieces, and 175,000 horses. Among those who accompany him, Ney cannot find more than 1,500 able to fight; of its own 3rd Army Corps there are only 300 men left, 100 of them able to fight will be the last to cross the Niemen, at around 8:00 p.m. In the Lithuanian forests there are still French troops and allied laggards, less than 30,000 soldiers grouped around the 10th Corps of MacDonald and the escorts of Murat and Eugene de Beauharnais, who will be retreating to Prussia until the end of the month, thousands of them will be buried in common graves after dying of extreme cold and starvation; some 6,000 survivors will escape to Prussia; the Schwarzenberg Corps will get back to its homeland. The disaster of the Grande Armée in Russia undermines the myth of Napoleon's infallibility: whoever his kingdoms were allies or subjugated will turn against him. Tsar Alexander I will prepare his armies to carry out a counter-offensive. During the "Patriotic War", some 250,000 Russian soldiers and 50,000 Cossacks have been killed; not counting the civilian casualties and their properties burned or looted by both sides.

15- South America: After a brief stay in Curaçao, Simon Bolivar had gone to New Granada, where he was placed in command of a garrison of 70 men in the small town of Barrancas. Intervening in small actions, was acquiring military prestige, until Colonel Manuel del Castillo requested his help to stop the realists who threatened to enter from Venezuela. Bolivar considered opportune to request permission to the government of Cartagena de Indias (on which his troops depended) before intervening in Venezuelan territory. To this end, he wrote the interesting manifesto of Cartagena, in which he also analyzes the causes of the defeat of the Venezuelan independence fighters against the Spaniards. Bolivar declares himself a centralist and blames federalism for much of the blame for the Venezuelan failure.

16- Río de la Plata: the royalist forces of Montevideo are defeated in the salting of Santa Lucia.

18 - Bonaparte enters Paris, the next day he will arrive at the Tuileries.

20- The first volume of Grimm's' Fairy Tales is published in Germany.

21- Arabia: the Egyptian Mehmet Ali conquers Mecca to the Wahhabis.

22- North America: the earthquake of Santa Barbara, followed by tsunami, destroys this mission and significantly damages the missions of Santa Ines and La Purísima Concepción, all in Alta California.

25- London: the British physicist Thomas Young proposes a universal phonetic alphabet, had studied the grammar and vocabulary of 400 languages and coined the Indo-European term to refer to a very large family of languages that presumably derived from a common language.

26- South America: Bolivar writes the "Manifesto of Cartagena", in which he asks for help to liberate Venezuela, then leaves this Colombian city liberated from Spanish power and gets his first victory in the battle of Tenerife, occupying Mompós and Guamal.

27 - Combat of Kelm. United States: the Bishop James Madison Society is founded at the College of William & Mary, Williamsburg, Virginia.

28 – Combat of Tilsit.

29- The war between the United States and Great Britain followed an irregular course. On the one hand, the attempted invasion of Canada was a failure, mainly because of the ineptitude of the US generals, but on the other hand the United States was surprisingly victorious in the naval clashes. This morning the Constitution destroyed the British ship Java off the coast of Brazil. Great Britain could say that it was using the bulk of its armada against France in Europe, but even so, the losses of warships to the United States humiliated the Royal Navy.

30 - An armistice is signed in the Lithuanian city of Tauroggen between the Prussian general Von Yorck, of the 10th Army Corps of the Grande Armée, and General Zabalkansky, of the Russian Army; he had cut off the Prussian supply route two weeks earlier, sentencing his fate. Signed without the knowledge of the Tsar and the King of Prussia, the Tauroggen pact was a betrayal of the French, but thanks to him all the Prussian soldiers could return alive. For this reason, in Prussia the agreement is welcomed with great satisfaction by the people, since it is understood as a breach of servility to Bonaparte, serving as an excuse to criticize in public the despotic hegemony of the French Empire.

31- South America: the royalists besieged in Montevideo attacked their adversaries with 2,300 men, while Rondeau only had a thousand soldiers. Thus the so-called battle of the Cerrito was fought; the royalists had to return to the city with significant casualties.

1813

JANUARY

1- Persia: the Russians take the city of Lankaran from the Persians; the Persian government begins negotiations for a peace treaty.

3- Napoleon orders his brother Joseph to leave Madrid and retreat to Valladolid to secure the northwestern peninsular, giving already lost the southwestern Spanish, given the disadvantageous situation of their forces. After hearing the news of the annihilation of the Grande Armée at the end of last year, Joseph, king of Spain, offers his brother Napoleon several of his occupation troops.

5- Pacific: Captain Maximilian Sanchez Correa travels to Hawaii and signs a treaty of friendship and trade with King Kamehameha I, who has unified the archipelago.

8- - South America: Simon Bolivar takes the royalists the city of Ocaña, in New Granada, near the border with Venezuela.

9- South America: Antonio Nariño defeats the federalists in Bogota and the United Provinces of New Granada submit to a central government.

10- Mexico: Mayor José de la Cruz founds a Casa de la Moneda (House of coin) of Guadalajara.

11- South America: a Venezuelan named Santiago Mariño, who had been exiled to the island of Trinidad, met in Chacachacare with 44 revolutionaries and planned to liberate eastern Venezuela from Spanish rule. The next day he will disembark in his homeland with an army.

13- Caribbean: Undersecretary of the Treasury Alejandro Ramirez, appointed first mayor of Puerto Rico, arrives at the island, where Mexican officials no longer arrive, forcing the governor to issue paper money and open the ports to trade with the rest of the world and to found the Economic Society of Friends of the Country, which will promote education.

14- South America: during the so-called coastal defense campaign, an Argentine militia defeats and captures a Spanish fleet of 3 ships, in the El Bellaco creek, near Gualeguaychu.

15- South America: the patriot Santiago Mariño organized during his exile in Trinidad a meeting to invade the Venezuelan east, this morning sails from the island of Chacachacare (officially British) and occupies with his small army the defenseless port of Güiria, Sucre.

16- Murat arrived in Poznan with the remains of the Grande Armée. There he put Eugène de Beauharnais in charge and marched to Naples to organize resistance against a possible Austrian invasion.

18- United States: after the surrender of Hull in Detroit, William Henry Harrison was put in charge of the army in the Northwestern United States. Willing to recover Detroit, he divided his army into two columns one under his command and the other under General James Winchester. He had orders not to get too far from Harrison, but, disgusted that he hadn't received the command of the operation he took the initiative and set out for Frenchtown, which had recently been taken over by the British. This afternoon take the city without effort.

21- Russian troops begin the siege of Danzig.

22- United States: General James Winchester's camp is attacked by surprise by an army of British and Indians under the command of General Henry Procter and Tecumseh. Almost half of his men died and most of the rest were taken prisoner.

23- United States: the British were not in a position to care for the prisoners captured the previous day and released them this morning, shortly after the Indians attacked and killed more than fifty of them, mostly wounded who could not fight. This will be remembered as the massacre of the Raisin River. Most of the victims were from the State of Kentucky, where nine cities today bear the names of officers killed in the massacre. Remember the Raisin! it will become the war cry of Kentucky militiamen.

24- South America: sent by the viceroy with 2,400 soldiers and 5 brigantines, Brigadier Antonio Pareja disembarks in San Carlos de Chiloe to conquer Chile, leaning on the southern regions, little sympathizers of independence.

25 - Concordat of Fontainebleu between Napoleon Bonaparte and Pope Pius VII: Napoleon finally succeeds in getting Pope Pius VII to sign a new concordat by which he abdicates his temporal authority in favor of Napoleon and cedes even part of his spiritual authority to the French bishops. He also agrees to fix the papal residence in Paris.

26- - England: The Mexican Dominican Servando Teresa de Mier, condemned to exile, imprisoned and fugitive, publishes in London his "History of the Revolution of New Spain", under the pseudonym of José Guerra, in which he defends the right to independence of the kingdoms created by Spaniards and natives in America.

27- Spain: combat of Mendivil.

28 – England: Pride and Prejudice is published, signed by the author of Sense and Sensibility, Jane Austen. It is one of the first romantic comedies in the history of the novel, whose first phrase has become famous. "It is a globally recognized truth that a single man, who owns a great fortune, needs a wife." His success was much greater than that of Sense and Sensibility.

29- South America: shooting in Pasto, Colombia, of the Colombian patriot Joaquin Caicedo y Cuero and of Alexander Macaulay, an American soldier in the service of the Colombian separatists, by order of the president of the Audience de Quito, Toribio Montes.

30 - Zeycz agreement, non-belligerence between Austrians and Russians.

31- South America: the second River Plate triumvirate convened a General Constituent Assembly, charged with drafting a Constitution for the United Provinces of the Rio de la Plata. The Constituent Assembly or Assembly of the year XIII, with Carlos de Alvear as its first president, also assumes a certain legislative and executive power, restricting the authority of the triumvirate, decrees the freedom of the children of the slave (freedom of bellies) and freedom of male slaves at 20 years old and at 16 years old women, or when they get married.

FEBRUARY -1813

1- United States: deprived of a good part of its forces, Harrison leaves its plans to attack Detroit and prepares to defend Ohio, ordering the construction of Fort Meigs.

2- Prussia: in Königsberg, the Prussian Landtag calls to arms against the French, who subdue the kingdom from 1807, when they disbanded their army; the act is instigated by Baron Von Stein, Minister of State of King Frederick William III, whom he intends to press with this action to convince him to officially abandon his forced military alliance with France, contracted last year, and already practically broken. A large part of the Germans are in favor of fighting for their independence, fed up with the abuses and impositions of the occupying troops. While the French survivors are resettled in Poznan, the Prussian Army reorganizes under General Blücher, with recruits from all the States of the Rhine Confederation. In cities like Berlin, hundreds of volunteers are presented daily. The core of the new army will be the 20,000 soldiers of General Yorck, who will soon join the Russian Cossacks of General Wittengstein, who will continue the persecution of the Grande Armée. South America: the revolutionary Junta of Quibdó, Colombia, calls an open town hall, proclaiming the absolute independence of Spain.

3- South America: José de San Martín's horse grenadiers defeat a small royalist army that tried to cross the Paraná River in San Lorenzo. It was not a great feat, but San Martin earns the confidence of his compatriots.

5- United States: the earthquakes of the previous year had shocked many American Indian tribes. In particular, the Creeks were convinced that earth movements had to be some kind of message from the spirits, but they differed in their interpretation. Some considered it a warning to return to their old way of life, prior to the arrival of white men. Tensions increased when a group of seven warriors killed two families of American settlers along the Ohio River. The Americans asked the Creeks to hand over the seven responsible, but the Indian chiefs thought it appropriate to execute them themselves, and when they did, a civil war broke out among the Creeks.

7- South America: the patriots of Gregorio Samaniego beat the Spaniards in the first fight of the Paranacito, in Argentina.

8- Spain: the guerrilla leader Espoz y Mina besieges the city of Tafalla, guarded by 400 French soldiers; General Abbé, French governor of Pamplona, sends reinforcements to the city.

9- Spain: the guerrilla Mina defeats in Tiebas the French forces sent in aid to the besieged of Tafalla. In Prussia: Major Adolf von Lützow, asks permission to King Frederick William III to form a volunteer militia. This soldier is a veteran of the campaign of 1807, when he participated in the battle of Auerstadt. After the dissolution of the national army by the French, von Lützow was part of an uprising the following year, being retired from active service, until the king restituted it in 1811.

10- Spain: Assault of Tafalla, the garrison, knowing that it would not receive aid, surrenders after the Spaniards open a breach with their artillery and prepare to assault the city. All the French are captured. After rendered Tafalla, Mina will assail Sos, although his garrison will escape. Generals Abbé and Claussel will begin to persecute him with all his troops.

11 – Spain: Combat of Poza.

12- Barclay de Tolly returns to the Russian Army as general of the 3rd Army.

13- South America: the brigadier Antonio Pareja advances in Chile defeats the garrison of Talcahuano and occupies this city and Concepción, despite the fierce defense of Chepe's fort.

15- The King of Prussia, Frederick William III, sends an ultimatum to Napoleon, demanding that he withdraw his troops from Prussia and pay compensation of 93 million francs for the years of occupation.

16 Prussia: the king agrees to Lützow's request, founding the Royal Free Prussian Corps, who will wear a black uniform instead of the traditional dark blue of the Prussian Army, as this is more expensive. The king will only provide them with weapons that they cannot obtain by other means. The Free Corps will awaken the patriotic fervor of tens of thousands of Germans, and will be the symbol of their struggle for independence. Many French will leave their urban garrisons just to see them arrive.

19- South America: the 3,000 men of Belgrano again defeat the 2,500 of Pio Tristan in Salta, capturing Tristan, with 2 generals, 7 chiefs, 117 officers and more than 2,000 soldiers: Esteban Agustin Gascon, soul of the uprising of 1809 in Chuquisaca, is appointed Governor of Salta and shortly after President of the Audience de Charcas by the Argentine government.

20 – Spain: brief Harrison offensive in Bejar. Prussia: in Lange Brücke, Berlin saboteurs disable several French cannons.

21- South America: the armies of Manuel Belgrano and Pio Tristan met again, this time in Salta, where Tristan was forced to capitulate. The royalist soldiers were released under oath that they would not take up arms against the United Provinces. As a consequence of this victory, the provinces of Chuquisaca, Potosí and, later, Cochabamba, in Upper Peru, rebelled against the Spaniards. Goyeneche resigned and shortly after returned to Spain. José Fernando de Abascal, the viceroy of Peru, appointed Joaquin de la Pezuela in his place. On the other hand Antonio Pareja was appointed captain general of Chile and sent him to the front of an army to quell the independence insurrections.

23- United States: the North American ship Hornet, under the command of Captain James Lawrence, sank the British ship Peacock in front of British Guiana.

24 – Germany: the citizens of Hamburg besiege the French garrison of the city.

25- South America: Grenadier Lieutenant Miguel Escobar seizes 2 royalist boats on an island next to Concepción del Uruguay.

26- South America: Simon Bolívar defeats the Spaniards and takes the city of Cucuta.

28 - Poland: in Kalisz, after several days of talks, King Frederick William III of Prussia and Tsar Alexander I of Russia sign an Alliance against the armies of Napoleon. The first objective of the new allies will be the expulsion of the French from German lands. This treaty will be the basis for constituting a new European grand coalition against the French Empire.

Luddism was a movement of English spinning and weaving workers, active in the early nineteenth century, at the beginning of the Industrial Revolution, and which became notable for the destruction of machines as a form of protest. The Luddites considered that machinery was used "in a fraudulent and deceptive way" to circumvent traditional labor practices. At first, Luddite attacks were shot by machine owners. After all the movement was repressed by military forces, and the hardening of British legislation resulted in severe penalties for the movement's participants.

MARCH-1813

1- Luddism is spread across Britain, now it reaches the county of Lancashire. In various places there were real battles between the army and the Luddites, which continued with their attacks against businessmen and magistrates. Some entrepreneurs built secret chambers in their buildings, to serve as a hiding place in case of an attack. Eighteen Luddites will be executed this year.

2- South America: Simon Bolívar occupies the plaza of San Antonio de Táchira, in Venezuela. The Congress of New Granada names him brigadier and citizen of this State.

3- South America: the viceroy of New Spain, Francisco Javier Venegas, is deposed and replaced by Felix Maria Calleja. According to the constitution of Cadiz, he received the title of Political Chief Superior, instead of the title of viceroy.

4 – Spain: Wellesley, Marquis of Wellington, is proclaimed Knight of the Order of the Garter.

7- South America: Galician Pascual Ruiz Huidobro, who had supported the May Revolution in Buenos Aires, is now suspected because he is Spanish, so he is sent as an ambassador to Chile to support emancipation, but dies during the trip in Mendoza.

10 – Germany: begins the first siege of Torgau, in Saxony.

11 – Spain: assault of Fuenterrabía, Fermin de Leguia, sergeant of Espoz and Mina, plans to attack the French garrison of the castle of Fuenterrabia. This afternoon he leaves Vera with only 15 men armed with his weapons, nails and ropes, and climbs the wall of the fortress with one of his companions at around 11:00 p.m. The French sentinels are surprised and disarmed, and after opening the main gate to the others, they disable the castle's artillery with the nails, throw many bullets into the sea, steal several barrels of gunpowder and a flag, to finally set fire to the fortress and flee without the rest of the garrison could reach them. For this action Fermin will be promoted to the rank of lieutenant. Prussia: King Frederick William III of Prussia creates the Order of the Iron Cross (Eisenkreuz Ordnung) with its corresponding medal, which will be imposed on Germans who excel in combat, as a reward for their courage and sacrifice. This is the first decoration of German military history that can be granted to officers and soldiers. The appearance of the new order is announced today in the Schlesischen Zeitung.

12 - Germany: the cavalry of the Cossacks arrives in Hamburg, the French soldiers withdraw.

13 – Spain: combat of Cargante, the French general Claussel, march with the divisions of Palombini and Foy, in total about 10,000 soldiers, to take the fortified place of Castro Urdiales, which serves as a refuge for the guerrillas operating in Santander, Vizcaya, and part of Vitoria and Burgos, harassing all French units and convoys around their provincial capitals and the cities of Bilbao and Santoña.

14- Poland: the Russians had occupied the Grand Duchy of Warsaw after the French defeat. This morning Tsar Alexander I formed a provisional Supreme Council in his capital in which only two Poles participate.

15- South America: the captain general of Venezuela Domingo de Montverde makes public an office of the Secretary of War that orders to execute all the insurgents who dare to resist the troops of the king, and all those who have been employed or cooperated with the revolution must be tried and sentenced to death.

16 – Prussia: the Prussian Landtag declares itself in favor of the war against France.

17- Prussia: General Yorck, who at first had been formed by a council of war for the treaty of Tauroggen, became a hero and this morning he entered Berlin amid cheers, the same day as King Frederick William III of Prussia declares war on France.

18 – Spain: combats of Osma and San Millan.

19- Germany: the French cross to the western shore of the Elbe, reaching the territory of the Confederation of the Rhine and settle in Dresden. The population rebelled ten days before to prevent it, but a unit of Cuirassiers Saxons came to the aid of the garrison of the castle of Königstein, making it possible for the French police to arrest the rebels later.

20 - Germany: French troops destroy the old bridge in Dresden.

21 - Germany: The Cossacks arrive in Lübeck, the French soldiers withdraw.

22 – Spain: the siege of Castro Urdiales begins.

23- Napoleon marches with his army to Germany to face the coalition. While in France many began to question the advisability of continuing to support the emperor, his wife Maria Luisa of Austria remained firmly supportive, and promoted recruitment among the younger French, to form a Regiment that was known as the "Maria Luisa."

24 - Pope Pius VII recanted the Concordat de Fontainebleau and Napoleon returned to treat him as a prisoner of state.

25- Germany: the French withdraw from Dresden, before the arrival of General Blücher's Prussian troops, who enter the capital this afternoon.

26 - Germany: a detachment of gendarmes arrives in Lüneburg, called by the commander of the garrison alarmed by the existing tension, but the inhabitants take to the streets and expel the reinforcements. Spain: combat of Orgaz. Francisco Villa, with 2 companies of Volunteers of Catalonia and a cavalry squad of Hunters of Ubrique, about 320 men in total, is attacked by 800 French horsemen when he was heading to the town of Orgaz. Outnumbered, the Spaniards stay for a short time and then retreat in order to the San Andrés de Yebene's bridge, where two other companies of Spanish soldiers are stationed. Villa now has about 400 infantrymen, who with their heavy discharges of rifle manage to repel the French cavalry, retiring after suffering 150 casualties; the squad of Hispanic Hunters suffered about 40 casualties; among the infants there were only two injured. Villa, two captains and a squadron rider will be decorated by the Spanish Army with the Laureate Cross of San Fernando.

27 - Germany: more and more people rise up against the French occupying forces in the cities and refuse to supply them, with riots and riots taking place due to any incident involving French gendarmes or officials. Eugene de Beahuarnais, commanding all the French and allied forces in Prussia and the Confederation of the Rhine, evacuates the garrisons and regroups his men in Poznan, where the survivors of the Russian campaign were billeted; In total, it gathers about 14,000 gendarmes and soldiers. From there they retire to Magdeburg, where they receive 10,000 reinforcement soldiers, from Marshal Davout.

28- Prussia: Encouraged by the firm pro-independence wishes expressed by the Germans, the King of Prussia, Frederick William III, in his proclamation "An mein Volk", urges all citizens who enlist in the Prussian Army, to fight against the French Empire . With this risky decision, the monarch is definitely united to the will of his subjects, demonstrated in energetic anti-

French popular revolts during this month, ready to lead their struggle for independence. The other German states begin to recruit battalions of volunteers for the war. The Czar Alexander I of Russia sends in its aid to the Army of the general Wittengstein, integrated in its majority by Cossacks that already march by the east of Prussia. England contributes by unloading thousands of rifles, uniforms and a lot of money; almost all good quality German equipment will be British. The improvised Prussian Army has 20,000 veteran soldiers of the Russian campaign, and will reach 100,000 militants and volunteers, but the real treasury cannot equip them regularly, allowing many to dress their peasant clothes or carry farm implements and weapons hunting. To pay for more armaments, impedimenta and supplies, the king needs public donations. German civilians contribute what they can to the cause: women deliver 160,000 gold rings; during these days the weddings will be performed with iron rings. Some donate their monthly salary, their horses, sell or pawn goods to donate the money. In total, the costs will raise about 6.5 million Thaler. In short, the Prussians will liberate Mecklenburg from the French, already retreating west of the Elbe, thus initiating the Befreiungskriege or the Wars of Liberation.

29- South America: the Biscayan royalist leader Antonio Zuazola defeats the patriotic guerrillas in Los Magüeyes, near Aragua de Maturin, in Venezuela, composed of farmers and ranchers in the area, and offers them a pardon if they return to the town, but As they do, it cuts off their ears, murders them and throws them into Inozua's lagoon, since the governor of Cumana pays a heavy peso for each insurgent ear.

30- North America: in Texas the revolutionaries of Bernardo Gutierrez de Lara pursue the governor Manuel de Salcedo and Lieutenant Colonel Simon de Herrera and defeat them in the Rosillo stream, the Indians being the ones who kill the most royalists (330 against only 6 republicans) by feeding on those who flee.

31 – Spain: in Lerin, Espoz and Mina attacks a detachment in march, capturing 300 French.

APRIL-1813

1- Germany: the gendarmes return to Lüneburg with 2,300 Saxon allies. The enraged civilians try to prevent them from entering, but the soldiers' rifles and artillery disarm them; several are killed and 50 are imprisoned; they and the rest of the citizens wait to suffer harsh reprisals, like imminent summary executions. The King of Prussia, hearing of the desperate situation in Lüneburg, sends a battalion of Pomeranian soldiers, who march throughout the day and night traveling about 50 km in less than 24 hours. They are joined by the Free Corps of General Lützow, about 2,000 men, and another 2,000 Cossacks arrived from Settin. Mexico: Bernardo Gutierrez de Lara, having failed in his attempt to implicate the United States in the independence of Mexico, had recruited an army of mercenaries through an advertisement in a Louisiana newspaper and with him had gone to Texas. After obtaining several victories, it obtained the surrender of the governor Manuel Maria de Salcedo. He was tried and sentenced to death along with other realists.

2 - Germany: in Lüneburg, before the imminent arrival of Freikorps and the Cossacks of General Wittgenstein to their city, the inhabitants rise up against the French garrison, armed with picks, shovels and other tools. The French army had retreated to the west, leaving the Lüneburg garrison isolated, and this afternoon Wittgenstein's troops assaulted the walls and gates of Lüneburg; after a hand-to-hand combat, the attackers enter the interior of the city, engaging in fierce clashes in the streets and squares; finally the Cossacks lancers break the closed formations of French and Saxon infantry. About 2,000 of them are taken prisoner, with their general and three banners.

3- Germany: the unexpected war against Prussia frustrated Napoleon's plans to rebuild a large army and invade Russia again. Since 1806 a large part of its troops were composed of soldiers from allied states, and it was they who suffered the greatest casualties in the wars, France still has a new generation of young people, an intact military infrastructure and a strong economy. Between 1811 and 1812, Napoleon had created a new National Guard, with the mission of defending French borders, and now Bonaparte will use them for the campaign against Prussia. In addition, Napoleon orders the recruitment in the States of the Confederation of the Rhine and Italy, which bring more men to the Grande Armée, to collect a total of some 400,000 soldiers at the end of March, fully equipped.

4 - Marshal Kutuzov dies; Wittgenstein is the new commander of the Russian 1st Army.

5 - The Prussian Freikorps invade the Kingdom of Saxony. Río de la Plata: Artigas gathers in the outskirts of the besieged Montevideo the first representative Congress of the peoples of the Eastern Provinces, where the "Instructions of the year XIII" will be drafted, Magna Carta of River Plate federalism.

6- Mexico: Gutierrez de Lara declares the independence of Texas, proclaims a Constitution appoints himself president of Texas in San Antonio. The execution of the realists was frowned upon by many of his followers, who withdrew their support, including José Alvarez de Toledo and Dubois and also many of the American mercenaries, who returned to their country. In Chile the patriot general Bernardo O'Higgins takes Linares.

7- South America: Antonio Nicolas Briceño "the Devil", had organized this year a small Venezuelan patriotic military force, after publishing in San Cristobal a side declaring "the war without quarter", he shot 2 Spaniards who had mocked and signed documents for Bolívar with his blood. He will launch an offensive towards Guasdualito in mid-May where he will be defeated by the royalist leader José Antonio Yáñez, who will take him prisoner with 12 officers and will be shot in Barinas.

8- North America: the Comanche intensify their attacks to San Jose de Palafox, in Texas, so a small fort is built and Governor Antonio Cordero and Bustamante recommend the city's inhabitants to abandon it, however many will remain there until 1818.

10- Spain: in Murcia and Alicante, Elío's Spanish 2nd Army, the Whittingham division and the Anglo-Sicilian column of Murray maneuver to meet and form a contingent with which to effectively harass the French invaders. To prevent this, French Marshal Suchet concentrates part of his forces at Fuente de la Higuera. Tonight Suchet goes with the division of General Habert to Caudete and sends General Harispe's division to Yecla, where the Spanish division of General Miyares is stationed, which he believed to be the weakest of the Allied deployment, despite having 4,000 soldiers.

11 – Spain: Battles of Yecla and Villena: during the dawn, the troops of Harispe march with stealth and at dawn they attack with total surprise the Spaniards in Yecla, engaging in a street fight. Miyares orders withdrawal to Jumilla, covering it the regiments of Burgos and Cadiz, that exceeded by the French in the streets of the town, they are enclosed in a chapel to continue the defense and to allow the rest of the Hispanics to retreat. Hiraspe continued assaulting the Spanish rear, while the infantry of Miyares retreated in good by the heights of the zone, yielding little by little terrain. But the French finally break their center, and all the Spanish soldiers are disbanded, being massacred by their persecutors; about 1,000 decide to surrender. At nightfall, Suchet marches with the division of Habert to the fortified town of Villena, guarded by the Spanish regiment of Velez Malaga, of 1,000 men. The British cavalry tries to stop him, but the French arrive at the village, knock down the doors with their artillery and the Spanish of the castle put down their weapons.

12 – Spain: combat of Biar, in Valencia. Marshal Suchet, after defeating the Spaniards in Yecla and Villena, attacked the troops of the English vanguard in Biar, commanded by Adam, when they were heading towards Castalla to meet with the other allies. The English defended themselves until the night, being able to fall back in order towards their destiny after sunset. Mexico: Jose Maria Morelos finally conquered Acapulco, although the Spanish garrison of San Diego fort will not capitulate until August.

13 – Spain: second battle of Castalla. At dawn, the British general Murray regroups some 17,000 allies in Castalla and deploys them in a line around the population. The division of Whittingham with the troops of Adam is placed in the left flank, on the top of a rugged hill, and in the right flank the division of Clinton is entrenched. In town he will be defended by the Mackenzie division; the three Spanish battalions of Roche remain in reserve. At dawn, Suchet arrives from Biar, deploying his 15,000 soldiers to Castalla. First he sends cavalry detachments to explore allied formations and then orders to attack his left flank. The Whittingham Mallorcan fight firmly reinforced by more Spaniards coming from Alcoy under Romero. The French colonel who led the charge, D'Arbod, is killed in the fight, and Suchet sends to the sector another four battalions commanded by General Robert, who are similarly rejected by the Anglo-Spanish soldiers, who also send more reinforcements to the army zone, with the attackers retreating down the hill. The French make trial attacks on the center and the allied right, but the Anglo-Sicilians remain in their posts and repel all attacks. Suchet realizing the solidity of the allied positions, orders a stepped retreat; Murray sends his men to the counterattack, advancing the Allied infantry from his left flank in two lines, and the cavalry from the right. Suchet retires through the Biar gorge to its barracks in Fuente de la Higuera and Onteniente; the allies stop chasing them and return to Castalla. During this day, the French have suffered about 1,000 casualties, although Murray will report having caused some 3,000; on the other hand, the allies had about 600.

14- United States: James Wilkinson occupies the island Delfina claimed from 1803, to avoid its use by the British, and Spain gives it to him. With it as a naval base, Wilkinson has no difficulty in conquering Mobile Fort in Alabama, whose district will be annexed to the Mississippi Territory, thus completing the incorporation of Spanish Western Florida.

15- Germany: 200,000 French, Italian and German troops are concentrated between the Elbe rivers, threatening Berlin, and Saale, near Dresden, east of the Confederation of the Rhine. The Army Corps of Eugene, the Lauristons, the 11th of MacDonald and the Regnier are located in the lower Saale, the 3rd of Ney in front of Weimar, the 6th of Marmont in Gotha, the 4th of Bertrand in Saafeld, and that of Oudinot in Coburg. Near them, in Magdeburg and on the banks of the Elbe, there is a body of Prussians and Russians watching over them, the rest of Blücher's allied army and Wittgenstein is camped near Dresden, protecting the Prussian border. The allies have about 100,000 soldiers.

17 - The Prussian Freikorps arrive in Leipzig, capital of Saxony.

19- South America: the viceroy appoints General Joaquin de La Pezuela to replace the defeated Goyeneche at the head of the army of Upper Peru.

20- Mexico: the 1,000 insurgents of General Mariano Matamoros beat Lieutenant Colonel Manuel Servando Dambrini, who was retreating to Guatemala, in the village of La Chincúa, in Chiapas; he takes refuge in Tonalá, but Matamoros, who has been wounded in one leg, forces him to surrender and shoots all the Spaniards in Paredón Bay, obtaining for this success the rank of lieutenant general.

21 – Spain: In Mendigorría, Espoz y Mina captures a French detachment.

23- South America: in Chile the brigadier Antonio Pareja advances victorious towards Yerbas Buenas, near Talca.

24- United States: James Procter and Tecumseh put under siege Fort Meigs and Harrison prepared to resist.

25- Germany: Napoleon arrives escorted by his Guard to Erfurt, at the center of the French deployment, and takes command of the Grande Armée, finding little information on allied positions. He soon orders the advance of all his troops to Merseburg and Leipzig. Today, the French cross the Saale through Weissenfels and invade Saxony, arriving in the early morning at Lützen, being attacked by the Russian vanguard.

26- Mexico: Jose Maria Morelos had disseminated among the Mexican insurgents a draft Constitution that summarized in thirty-eight points known as Constitutional Elements.

27- South America: the Chilean dictator, Jose Miguel Carrera, organized an army of 9,000 men under the command of Juan de Dios Puga and sent him against the army of Pareja, who was advancing from the north. Tonight Puga attacked the royalists by surprise near the village of Yerbas Buenas, but as soon as the sun came out and the Spaniards could see their attackers they reacted and took the victory. Among the casualties was Puga himself.

28- United States: an American fleet of fourteen ships arrived across the Eire Lake until the coasts of York, in Canada. In command was General Henry Dearborn. This afternoon the battle of York was fought, in which the Americans won. However, they could not capture the British fleet and take control of the lake. Moreover, while the capitulation was being negotiated, the Americans pillaged, looting and setting fire to numerous buildings.

29-South America: Juan Jose Pasos is replaced by Jose Julian Perez in the River Plate triumvirate.

30- Germany: French troops invade Saxony.

MAY-1813

1- Spain: combat of Poserna, death of the French marshal Bessieres.

2 - Germany: Battle of Lützen or Gross Görschen. Napoleon sends to the east the Army Corps of Lauriston, supported by the Cavalry Corps of Latour Mabourg, with the aim of taking Leipzig, the capital of Saxony; while the 11th MacDonald Corps advances towards Markranstadt and the 3rd Corps of Ney marches on its right towards Lutzen, where it must meet with the troops of the Guard, after it goes the 6th Corps of Marmont, with the Corps of Bertrand covering its right flank, more to the southwest, heading to Tachau. The allies congregate southeast of Lützen and the environs of Pagau and Zwenkau. The Prussians, led by Blücher, have three brigades, two from Upper and Lower Silesia and another from Brandenburg, the divisions of Hunerbein and Steinmetz and a cavalry reserve. The Russians, commanded by Wittgenstein, contribute the 2nd Army Corps, the 3rd Corps, of Grenadiers, and the 5th Corps, of the Guard, plus three regiments of Cossacks, and a reserve of cavalry. In total they add about 100,000 men. Wittgenstein, commanding the entire allied contingent, decides to attack the French who go to Lützen and the Elster River, because they seem less numerous. Blucher, at the vanguard of the Allied army, marches with the three regiments of Cossacks and another of Prussian light cavalry being south of Kaja, at 09:00 am., two divisions of the 3rd Corps of Ney, in turn in the vanguard of the army French. While Blücher waits for more allied troops, Ney orders his 20,000 men to occupy defensive positions in the vicinity. Around 11:00 am, some 73,000 Russians and Prussians attack them, but the French have entrenched themselves in the five villages south of Lützen and are bitterly opposed despite their inferiority; almost all the Allied army is then in the vicinity of Lützen. Napoleon, who had sent Ney far ahead so that the allies would think him weak and attack him, was then admiring a statue in memory of King Gustav Adolph of Sweden, when he heard the noise of cannons. He immediately comes to the aid of Ney with the cavalry of his Guard, and sends messengers to the nearby French Corps, so that they converge from the north towards Lützen. While the divisions of Ney fight fiercely, losing and recovering the peoples they defend, Napoleon arrives on the battlefield with the cavalry of his Guard, and throughout the morning the divisions of the 4th Corps of Bertrand, the infantry and artillery of the Guard, the 11th Corps of MacDonald, and the 1st Cavalry Corps of Lateur Mabourg, the French gathering about 110,000 soldiers in the area, counterattacking with such speed that they surprise Wittgenstein. The allies, outnumbered and pressured by their flanks, form in two lines with their backs to Lützen; the first formed by the Prussian brigades and the second with the other two Prussian divisions and two divisions of Russian grenadiers and riflemen; the rest of the Russian army is in reserve, for lack of space to maneuver. Napoleon deploys 100 cannon before the allies, which wreak havoc in the center of the first line, opening a large gap; then he sends his reserves to the front to carry out an infantry charge and break the second Prussian line. The allies retreat in order, for the French cannot harass them because they lack sufficient cavalry and their infantry is exhausted by continuous marches and combat. In the early afternoon, the King of Prussia and the Tsar decide to withdraw their troops, against the opinion of Blücher. The allies retreat to the south of Lützen after suffering some 18,000 casualties, the French have some 20,000. Bonaparte will say: "- The Prussians have finally learned that they are no longer the soldiers of Frederick the Great ..." To some extent, the victory is due to the fact that the Germans have improvised an army of peasants, both brave and inexperienced, what little they can do against the French veterans, who have been trained in the Napoleonic campaigns. Only the lack of cavalry has saved the allies from a final defeat.

3- Caribbean: Contrary to the terms of its capitulation, Francisco Miranda is imprisoned in the vaults of El Morro, in San Juan, Puerto Rico.

4 - Germany: combats of Möckern, Dannigkow, Vehlitz and Zeddenick: Ney attacks the enemy's rearguard.

5- South America: departure from Valparaiso, Chile, the merchant frigate "Pearl", armed by the Chileans with 22 cannons and the merchant brig "Potrillo, armed with 20 cannons, to face the Spanish corsair frigate" Warren ", but part of the crew of the "Pearl" rebels and delivers it to the Spaniards and together they capture the brig, which will be incorporated into the Navy.

6- United States: Harrison sent a messenger asking for reinforcements, and this morning a regiment arrived under Colonel William Dudley. At first it seemed that he was going to achieve his purpose of breaking the siege, but when the Indians fled in disarray, Dudley's men set out to chase them, abandoning the British artillery they had captured, and which was recovered by the Canadian militiamen. Procter reorganized the Indians of Tecumseh and managed to destroy the army of Dudley, whose men died, were captured or fled where they had arrived. When the battle was over, the Indians snatched some thirty American prisoners from the British and killed them. Procter did nothing to prevent it, and it had to be Tecumseh who ended the killing. He called Procter "woman" for not having prevented the massacre.

7- United States: the siege of Fort Meigs resumed, but most of the Indians had left and the Canadian militiamen wanted to do the same. Fearing to stay with fewer men than Harrison, Procter will abandon the siege two days later.

8- North America: Following the orders of its government, which fears a war against Spain, the United States Army would raise its flag in Fernandina and withdraw from Amelia Island and the occupied territories in Florida, returning to Georgia.

9 - Germany: Wittgenstein orders to evacuate the city of Dresden and destroy the only bridge that remained; when Napoleon arrives he cannot continue the pursuit, because the pontoons are far behind, advancing with the columns of infantry. Napoleon enters Dresden.

10- South America: the General Constituent Assembly of the United Provinces of the Río de la Plata adopts the Patriotic March as a national anthem. It had been composed by the Spaniard Blas Parera for a play premiered the previous year in Buenos Aires, although the lyrics were not the ones that were sung in it, but another composed by a spectator, Vicente Lopez. Parera refused to make some adaptations because he considered that the lyrics were offensive to Spain, but then he was imprisoned and threatened with the execution, so in one night he finished the score that the Assembly later approved. The anthem lasted about 20 minutes. The lyrics use the term "Argentines" to refer to the River Plate people, a name that would become usual due to the spread of the hymn.

11 – Spain: siege of Castro Urdiales. The coastal village of Castro Urdiales is guarded by 1,000 soldiers of the Iberia Regiment, commanded by Colonel Pedro Pablo Álvarez; its fortification consists only in an old wall provided with towers in some points, of little thickness. Luckily for the defenders, nearby are well-armed English ships anchored.

12 – Germany: end of the first siege of Torgau.

13- Germany: French engineers build a bridge in Dresden.

14- South America: Bolívar leaves from Cucuta, Colombia, to invade Venezuela, in the so-called "Admirable Campaign"

15- Asia: the Cambodian King Ang Chan returns to his country at the head of a Vietnamese army. His brothers had to flee to Bangkok and this day Ang Chan II enters the Cambodian capital and officially recovers his crown. Siam recognized the monarch in exchange for some territories.

16- South America: the Chilean army returned to face the Spanish, this time in San Carlos. The Chileans were led by José Miguel Carrera himself, while Antonio Pareja was ill and yielded to Juan Francisco Sanchez, who won a new victory. At nightfall the Chilean troops were scattered and disorganized.

17 – Spain: King Joseph Bonaparte leaves Madrid, initiating with his armies a campaign destined to occupy or block several port cities from which the allied troops under the command of Wellington, in total about 180,000 men, receive supplies thanks to the maritime superiority of the Royal Navy that also transports cash and materials, making landings and evacuations. José leaves the capital followed by a spectacular convoy of more than 2,000 carriages of all kinds, loaded with rich baggage, trunks with rich clothes, chests with jewels and money in Spanish and French currency, furniture and works of art; much of the looting and plundering of French troops during these years. He is also accompanied by thousands of courtiers, escorted by his Guard.

18 - Germany: the last French troops cross to the east bank of the Elbe, the invasion of Prussia begins. In Königswarta the French outposts of Napoleon reach the Prussian troops, fighting a series of skirmishes. South America: Antonio Pareja dies, the Captain General of Chile, was succeeded by Juan Francisco Sanchez, who was already replacing him during his illness.

19 – Prussia: battles of Bautzen and Würtzchen. The French pursue the withdrawal of allied troops, some 196,000 Prussians and Russians under Wittgenstein, who withdraw from Lützen to Prussia. The King of Prussia and the Tsar of Russia order their troops to form defensive in Bautzen, about 60 km northwest of Dresden, unfolding on a 10 km front, on two baselines, entrenching themselves in some villages and in the East bank of the river Spree. At midday about 115,000 French, most of the 3rd Corps of Marshal Ney, attack the 50,000 soldiers of the first allied line; They manage to cross the Spree, and after a bitter fight, they take Bautzen. But the French have little cavalry, causing relatively few casualties to the allies, who retreat maintaining their second line, and avoid defeat. At nightfall, Napoleon orders to attack the allies in a pincer maneuver: Ney in the north and Bonaparte himself in the south. But the arrival of the night makes the maneuvers difficult, and Ney leaves a lot of free space on his left flank, for which the Prussians and Russians try to escape from the encirclement. On the following day, both armies will continue to move and unfold; the allies reinforce their right wing.

20- Prussia: battles of Bautzen and Würtzchen, both armies continue to move and unfold; the allies reinforce their right wing. Spain: King Joseph arrives in Valladolid with his great convoy. South America: in Chile the brigadier Antonio Pareja dies of fever in Chillan, he is succeeded by Lieutenant Colonel Juan Francisco Sanchez.

21- Prussia: Napoleon gathers about 100,000 soldiers in the vicinity of Würtzchen, near Dresden, where Blücher, Sayn and Wittgenstein have a similar contingent. The French attack, engaging in bloody combat, each side losing 20% of its strength; at the end of the day the allies retire to the east, crossing the Oder River.

22- Prussia: In the morning the 96,000 Ney soldiers resume their attack to prevent the 90,000 allies near Bautzen from retreating; the second allied line attacks to cover the escape of the rest. Ney assaults the positions of the Allied right flank, finding great resistance in the village of Preititz, while Napoleon tries to send troops to support the attack. The French sink the Allied right flank, forcing the men of Blucher and Wittgenstein to retreat at 16:00 pm; but the bulk of the Allied army manages to get away from the battlefield, the others retreat to the rear, and due to the shortage of French cavalry, they manage to escape successfully. In Bautzen, the French have suffered 13,000 casualties and the allies 15,000; and in Würtzchen both armies had about 20,000 casualties. Napoleon is angry, because his troops have not taken prisoners, nor seized enemy cannons or flags; that's why he does not consider them victorious. He orders his commanders to immediately pursue the allied retreat to Silesia. Spain: siege of Castro Urdales. The French battalion, escorted by 100 horsemen, arrives at the walled square, deciding to take it by assault. Wellington begins the persecution of King Joseph, leaving Ciudad Rodrigo this morning.

23- Spain: tonight the attackers try to climb the walls; the garrison discovers them, and supported by the artillery of the British ships rejects the attack. South America: Bolivar enters Merida, where he is proclaimed "Liberator", title by which he will be remembered.

24- Spain: siege of Castro Urdales: the French batteries open a gap of about ten meters wide in the wall in front of the convent of San Francisco, damaging it too. The opening is assaulted by a column of Grenadiers, while two other Hunters begin to climb the walls. The Spanish manage to reject two consecutive rounds, but at the third the French come reinforced by another contingent, and cross the outer wall; the garrison retreats to the castle. While two companies contain the invaders and destroy all the war material, Alvarez and the rest of the regiment goes to the hermitage of Santa Ana, where they board the English ships and are evacuated. Finally, the French also climb the walls of the castle and surprise their defenders, killing almost everyone. Although the French general Foy will try to prevent it, Castro Urdiales will be looted and set on fire by his men.

Joseph I Bonaparte, king of Spain since 1808, had tried to carry out a reformist government with the help of Francophile intellectuals, Spanish admirers of the French Revolution, and although they approved measures such as the dissolution of the antiquated Court of the Holy

Inquisition, their number and sympathy for he was progressively diminishing, as he contemplated the abuses perpetrated by the invading armies. In fact, he was a liberal monarch who could undermine the foundations of the Old Regime if he had received popular support. He traveled a lot throughout the Spanish territory to get known and get it: during his 5 years of reign, he was in the capital at intervals, until adding 3 and a half years, the rest spent 1 year and a half in Valencia, and 7 months in capitals like Seville, Granada, Valladolid and Vitoria; the rest of the time, about 3 months, it would happen in more than 50 towns. I would only return to Paris for a month. During his stay in Madrid, the monarch demolished several convents and churches to make squares, parks and avenues, such as the squares of the East, the Cortes, Santa Ana, San Martin or Ramales, hence the town nicknamed him "Rey Plazuelas", although he is better known as "Pepe Botella" for his alleged love of alcoholic beverages. The people of Madrid repudiate him, and he himself never felt loved by the Spanish people. During the occupation, the people of Madrid went hungry. The fanega of wheat came to cost 540 reals and the baked bread of two pounds to 12 reals. The poorest had to feed on cabbages and herbs. Between September 1811 and July 1812, more than 20,000 citizens died of starvation.

25- Spain: the allies have 80,000 soldiers in southwestern Portugal, 50,000 British and 30,000 Lusos; Another 100,000 Spaniards are grouped into five armies in Spain: that of General Castaños, of which the guerrillas of Espoz y Mina, Longa and others are part, with 40,000 soldiers, deployed between Galicia, Asturias and the north of Castile and Leon; that of Copons, with 10,000 in Catalonia; that of Elio, with 20,000 in Murcia; that of the Duque del Parque with 12,000 in Sierra Morena, and O'Donell with 15,000 in Andalusia. Wellington finally manages to coordinate all the actions of its various allied forces, beginning in spring a campaign from Portugal against the French armies of Claussel, Drouet, d'Erlon, Gazán and Reille, when they were trying to subdue the Spanish guerrillas and soldiers in the areas of Vascongadas and Levante. Due to the shipments of troops to Napoleon, only about 115,000 French soldiers will remain in Spain by mid-year; so the French armies in the Iberian Peninsula are very weak. Although the armies of Joseph obtain some victories, the later advance of the numerous allied troops converts their offensive maneuvers in retreats. Finally, Napoleon asks his brother to withdraw from Spain, unable to send reinforcements, to need as many men as possible to battle the huge forces of the European Coalition. This is how the French withdrawal from the Iberian Peninsula will begin. South America: Captain General de Montverde had embarked in La Guairá with about 300 veterans and landed in Barcelona, where he increased his column to 2,000 men, with whom he tries to conquer Maturin, defended by Manuel Piar with 700 soldiers (one of which is Antonio José de Sucre, 18) of a total of 1,200 men. Montverde is defeated in the battle of the Alto de los Godos, where the patriot side highlights the participation of a battery of women, such as Juana Ramirez "The Advanced" and the Chaimas Indians of Punceres under the command of José Miguel Guanaguanay, who dies in combat.

26 - Prussia: Haynau combat. Napoleon orders his marshals to persecute the retreating allies, to prevent them from stopping and trying to counterattack. Because of the rush, commanders do not adopt tactical precautions, such as support between units or the scout patrol detachment. Blücher perceives the French neglect, and sends 20 squadrons of cavalry against the division of General Maisons, inflicting many casualties and forcing his infantry to retreat before being annihilated. This action raises the morale of the Landwehr, the Prussian Army and increases the sympathy of the German population. However, Wittgenstein and Blucher prefer to maintain a greater distance from the bulk of the French army. Napoleon begins to distrust the neutrality of Austria; crucial for its supply lines that extend vulnerable to the north of its border, so proposes an armistice to the allies, gaining time to ensure the Austrian loyalty and receive the long-awaited reinforcements of cavalry needed to continue the campaign. With nothing to lose, the allies will sign a truce of 6 weeks, probably one of the biggest mistakes of Bonaparte's career; because it allowed the King of Prussia to reorganize and increase his army, to which every day hundreds of volunteers join.

27- United States: Henry Dearborn had retired from York and, after allowing a rest to his troops in Fort Niagara, he set out to attack Fort George, located on the other side of Niagara, by Lake Ontario. He deployed an amphibious attack, with some 2,000 infantrymen and a fleet of fourteen ships, before which the British had to flee. Dearborn, instead of consolidating his position, launched himself in pursuit of the British.

28- Spain: the last French soldiers, the rear guard of Joseph's army, leave Madrid after making a last plunder of what little is left of its inhabitants. The French leave a city, and its province, materially and economically ruined. Wellington arrives in Salamanca.

29- Spain: Graham, leaving from the south of Braganza, to the north of Portugal, harasses the flank of the convoy of the king Jose, driving to the Army of Portugal of general Reille towards the northeast. United States: a British fleet, under the command of Lieutenant George Prevost, the governor of Canada, crossed Lake Ontario to attack Sacket's Harbor, in the State of New York. The attack began at dawn but the British ended up re-shipping wildly.

30 - Germany: beginning of the siege of Hamburg.

31 – Spain: Wellington crosses the Douro River, chasing the convoy of Joseph Bonaparte.

JUNE-1813

1- United States: James Lawrence was in command of the Chesapeake and encountered the British ship Shannon near Boston. Although the forces were balanced, the American crew was inexperienced and in fifteen minutes of bombing the Chesapeake was destroyed. Lawrence died in combat and his last words were "do not deliver the ship", but the ship was delivered.

2 – Prussia: the Armistice of Pleischwitz is signed between France, Prussia and Russia; end of the First Liberation War. In Spain: bloody combat in Morales.

3 – Prussia: in Roda the Freikorps liberate 200 German recruits who were prisoners of the French. Spain: the British general Murray temporarily besieges Tarragona. King Joseph Bonaparte leaves Valladolid heading to Palencia with a large convoy escorted by Marshal Jordan's troops.

4- Spain: Wellington chases King Joseph, the commander in chief of the Allied armies has in Portugal and eastern Spain with 112,000 soldiers. To harass the French convoy, he sends General Graham northward with 40,000 men, supported from a distance by the 12,000 Spaniards of the Andalusia Army, commanded by Giron, while he himself will pursue Joseph from the southwest with the rest of his army, looking to cut the withdrawal.

5- Sweden joined the Sixth Coalition and crown prince Charles John, that is, Bernadotte, who was Napoleon's marshal, took command of the Allied army in Prussia.

6 – Prussia: combat of Luckau. United States: Pursued by the Americans, the British decided to attack by surprise in Stoney Creek. Despite the fact that there were about 700, in front of 3,400 enemies, they managed to capture the US commanding officers, John Chandler and William Winder, who ended up surrendering. That same day Dearborn was relieved of command and his place was occupied by James Wilkinson. The Americans resigned to enter Canada and retired to Fort George.

7- North America: Juan Pablo Galeana del Río secures insurgent control of the Acapulco port in Mexico, by taking the island of La Roqueta tonight, capturing a group of royalist soldiers.

8- Germany: the Freikorps enter Bavaria, taking the city of Hof. Spain: the French general Paris, in command of the garrison of the Aragon capital, is ordered to evacuate his garrison and join the troops of Suchet in Mequinenza. This morning leaves the city, leaving a detachment of 500 men in the castle of Aljafería. At dusk Lancers of Castile regiments and the troops of José Duran enter the city.

9- Mexico: the landowner Julian Villagran, self-proclaimed "Julian I, Emperor of the Huaxteca", who had recruited an insurgent army of 4,000, is captured with 36 men in the ranch of San Juan Amaxac and shot with 22 of them in Gilitla.

10- South America: Simon Bolivar enters Merida, acclaimed by the population, the realistic forces fled before his arrival. Shortly after, he took Trujillo.

11- South America: Bolivar proclaims in Mérida his decree of War to Death, which establishes the death penalty for all Spaniards who do not actively participate in favor of Venezuelan independence.

12- South America: Captain Bartolommeo Lizón marches from Maracaibo with a thousand soldiers against San Antonio del Táchira, Venezuela, where Bolívar has left Captain Cayetano Redondo Moreno, commanding 660 men, who is defeated, captured, beheaded and quartered by order of Lizón, its members will be placed in the 4 sides of the town and its head, fried in oil, presented to its mother, Marta Moreno.

13- Prussia: Major Lützow, commander of the Royal Free Corps of Prussia, is officially informed of the armistice between Napoleon and King Frederick William III, having to return all the French soldiers he had captured and return to the eastern bank of the Elbe, on the border of the Kingdom of Bavaria, about 150 km east of where the Freikorps are located. Today, when they camp southwest of Leipzig, the French captured two detachments when they were looking for food and fodder. Lützow goes with a white flag to the Bavarian capital, with the intention of speaking with General Arreghi, commanding the French forces in the area, believing that they would have made a mistake. Citizens cheer the major all the way to the French quartering. Arreghi promises the Prussians that they will be able to reach the border without being attacked, but in the afternoon, a body of Dragons pursues the escort of Lützow shortly after leaving Leipzig, and while their commander attacks them, he tells the Prussian officer: " Truce for everyone, but not for you ...! " The Freikorps camp is surrounded, resulting in about 300 Prussians dead or imprisoned. Lützow, with the majority of the Prussians, escapes to Leipzig, being well received by the population, but they cannot help him. Napoleon declares that the Freikorps are not soldiers, but bandits, and whoever helps them will pay the consequences. The fugitives flee to the east, leaving behind their wounded, which will be captured by the French and condemned to forced labor in the south of France. Napoleon degrades Arreghi, and announces arrests and punishments against anyone who shows sympathy for the enemies of France. All weapons and food are seized; the city council of Leipzig must supply the French garrison of the Wittenberg fortress. When the authorities come to Bonaparte to protest, he insults them, refusing to assist them. Spain: Joseph Bonaparte leaves Burgos, alarmed by the proximity of Wellington's troops.

14- Spain: Espoz y Mina chases the troops of Marshal Paris, who is forced to change routes and flee to the French border, disobeying his orders. Even so, the men of Mina reach their rear in Alcubierre, and the terrified French abandon to the Hispanics all their artillery and baggage to lighten their flight to Huesca, and then, from Jaca, to enter their country.

15– The **SIXTH COALITION** is formed: in the town of Reichenbach the United Kingdom organizes a new military coalition against France made up of Prussia, Russia and Austria. Sweden will soon be added.

16- Spain: Josph plans to group his armies, which are in retreat from various points of the Peninsula, retreating to the Ebro River, to stay there until everyone joins him, and to that end establishes his barracks in Miranda del Ebro; the Army of the South marches between Salamanca and Ávila; the Center between Segovia and Valladolid; that of Portugal between Burgos and Pamplona, the Army of the North continues in the Vascongadas and Navarra, and the Army of the Noon in Valencia. Wellington continues to advance, after leaving Medina del Pomar it turns east, heading towards Vitoria to cut off the French fleeing route towards Bayonne, the shortest route to France.

17- Spain: Wellington establishes its quarters in Quincoces. When informed of this maneuver that may involve him from the north, King Joseph decides to establish a new containment line on the Zadora river, and heading northeast, this afternoon deploys his troops to Vitoria to protect his escape route, waiting for the arrival of the Army of the North, to the control of Claussel, that is more to the south, in Navarre, and the division of Foy, that operates in the north coast.

18 – Spain: combats of Osma and San Millán.

19- South America: the vanguard of Bolivar, under the command of Colonel Atanasio Girardot, defeats the royalists in Agua Obispo, thus clearing the ground for the advance of Bolivar.

20- Spain: Wellington locates its headquarters in Subijana de Morillas, about 8 km of the Zadora River and 20 km west of Vitoria; before him the French armies are deployed on the eastern bank of the river. King Joseph has three French armies: that of the South or Andalusia, with 34,000 soldiers, that of the Central Plateau or the Center, with 17,600 men, and that of Portugal, with 17,400 soldiers; In total about 60,000 infantry, 8,000 horsemen and 153 cannons, which the monarch places under the leadership of Marshal Jourdan who deploys them in a line of three leagues following the eastern margin of Zadora, from west to northwest of Vitoria, closing the roads to Bilbao, Bayonne, Logrono and Burgos. The Army of Portugal, commanded by the Count de Reille, will defend the right flank, north of Vitoria, between the hills of the towns of Abechuco, Gamarra Mayor and Gamarra Minor, following the channel of the Zadora. The Army of the Center, commanded by Drouet, Count d'Erlon, occupies the hill of Ariñez where he mounts a powerful battery, which beats the entire Zadora valley. The Army of the South, commanded by Gazan, is positioned on its left flank, occupying the heights of Puebla de Arganzón. During the night, the allied right, some 20,000 soldiers under General Hill, is positioned near Arganzón, in the south wing of French deployment. The allied center is directed by Wellington himself, with more than 30,000 Britons and almost all the artillery, west of Nanclares de Oca. But the allied left, 25,000 soldiers under Graham, is still far away, northwest of Vitoria, to cut the road to the divisions of Foy and Palombini that come from Vizcaya.

21- Spain: battle of Vitoria. Upon realizing that Claussel's army will not arrive for two days, Wellington decides to attack using his numerical superiority; it has 35,000 Englishmen, 27,000 Portuguese and 16,000 Spaniards near Vitoria; in total 68,000 infants, 10,000 horsemen and 96 cannons. General Giron could arrive shortly with the 12,000 Spaniards of the Andalusia Army, but Wellington prefers to attack without waiting for his arrival and observing from a hill near Nanclares and Villodas, he realizes that, in this sector, the French deployment is weak, with its units very separate, in addition there are several intact bridges over the Zadora, incomprehensibly Jourdan has not taken the precaution of destroying them. Wellington plans a pincer maneuver, attacking Joseph's troops in the southwest, crossing the Zadora River, and wrapping the enemy in the northwest of Vitoria, cutting off their possible escape routes to Bilbao and Bayonne. The Allied soldiers deploy parallel to the Zadora River; most of the British accompany Wellington in the center, the Spaniards are part of the armies of the flanks.

The confrontation occurs in three points, from the first hours of the morning to the middle of the afternoon: in the towns of Arganzón and Subijana, to the southwest of Vitoria and to the south of the battlefield; those of Gamarra and Achabuco, to the north; and in the towns of Ariñez and Zuazo, east of the capital, and at the center of the battle. Then there is a brief fight around Vitoria. At 07:30 hours the Allied right flank, composed of the 2nd British division of General Stewart, the Portuguese of the Count of Amarante and the Spanish of General Pablo Morillo, advance towards the hills of Puebla de Arganzón and the Las Conchas gorge, occupied by troops of the Army of the South, under Gazan. The Hispanics, at the vanguard of the assault, march through the undergrowth crossing the Zadora, and after a brief shooting, the French hunters retreat, but continue firing ambushed among the vegetation to then retreat and attack again. Around 08:00, the Spaniards take the heights close to Arganzón and clash with Marissin's riflemen, causing them to retreat; the rest of the French left flank recedes towards Subijana de Álava, further north. Morillo asks for reinforcements to Hill, but before they arrive, it loads against the French division, positioned in a hill and forces it to back down after a fierce fight; Morillo is slightly wounded, and British brigadier general Cadogan falls dead at 08:30. At 09:00, the 2nd British division crosses the river through Arganzón and attacks the French located in the hills; an hour later Gazan sends two reinforcement brigades to contain the Allied advance; but when they arrive they find very little room to maneuver, having given up their comrades too much ground, and cannot contain the enemy advance. Around 10:00 am, two British brigades and the Portuguese brigade of the 2nd British division occupy Subijana; half an hour later they try to advance against the hill of Ariñez, in the French center, but two other French brigades, with artillery support from the battery of the hill, make them go back towards the town. At 10:30, the Spanish regiments of Julian Sanchez "El Charro", Cortazar and Dos Pelos arrive from the south on the road from Logroño to Vitoria, trying to flank the French attacking the rear of their left flank. Towards 11:00 am Jourdan sends the division of Cassegnes and the division of Dragons of General Tilly, containing the Hispanics with artillery support; King Joseph himself goes to harangue his troops, exposing himself to the Allied fire. After a recess of the combat, the French realize several attacks trying to recover Subijana, but the men of Hill, well entrenched, reject them. At 1:30 p.m., the brigades of Hill's 2nd division advance slowly towards Arianez, pushing the French left flank against its central formation to the north. At midday the Spaniards are left without ammunition and go to the second line, the French have suffered many casualties throughout the morning. Towards 14:00, the French divisions of Villatte and Conroux withdraw their left flank towards Esquivel, pushed by the 2nd division of Hill and the Anglo-Spanish brigades of Morillo and Cadogan; further east, Cassagnes returns to the center of the battle to reinforce the French lines, leaving the left flank defended by the Dragons of Tilly, who retire to the north around 18:00 hours.

The allied left, composed of the 1st and 5th English divisions of Graham, the Spanish of Francisco Longa and the Portuguese brigade of Pack, arrive at Munguía around 07:00 hours, about 18 km northeast of Vitoria after a whole day of March. This distance is due to the fact that initially these troops were not destined to participate, not being able to reach the assigned area until 10:30 in the morning. Allied troops continue advancing until they stop a few kilometers north of Abechuco, considering that Graham's forces are far superior to his; therefore he decides to wait for the events in the center of the battlefield. At 11:00, Reille takes advantage of the passivity of the allies and withdraws to the south the three brigades that he held before Abechuco, leaving a brigade entrenched in the city and placing the others with the rest of his army, on the south bank of the Zadora. At midday Graham attacks in coordination with the troops of Wellington, who crossed the Zadora to the southwest. Graham divides his men into two columns; one will direct it against Abechuco and Gamarra Mayor, and the other, formed by the Spaniards under Longa, will march towards Gamarra Minor and Durana, northeast of Vitoria, to try to control the Bayonne road. Meanwhile, Graham divides his column; the 1st division of Howard advances towards Abechuco with support of Portuguese cavalry, and the 5ª and 6ª divisions of Oswald and Pack, with the Portuguese of Beresford, will have to take Greater Gamarra, in the French right flank. Reille sends to the division of Lamartiniere to reinforce the brigade and defend this town. At 12:30, a hard fight begins in Abechuco and Gamarra Mayor. The French oppose great resistance to being well protected in houses, barricades and walls. The English and Portuguese divisions carry out several charges to the bayonet, but the defenders reject them with rifle discharges, sometimes fired at point-blank range; the allies take some houses but the fight will last for about three and a half hours. Meanwhile, the Spanish division of Longa heads to Gamarra Minor, skirting the hills of Aroca through some woods, and dodging the French defenders, arrives at the town, where the division of General Casapalacios, formed by Spanish supporters of King Joseph, retires without fighting south of the Zadora, despite having the support of the French cavalry brigade of Curto. At 1:30 p.m. the Spaniards of Longa are positioned north of Durana, on the French left flank, cutting the route of Joseph's convoy to Bayonne. Half an hour later they evict the French from the village with a load of bayonets. From 2:00 pm., Reille regroups his troops and makes up to three ferocious counterattacks to avoid the loss of Gamarra Mayor and Abechuco. The French assaults fail in their attempt to expel the allies, already well encapsulated in the periphery of the populations. Between 3:00 and 4:00 pm, the Anglo-Portuguese troops of Graham evict Lamartiniere de Gamarra's division after a bloody hand-to-hand combat; however they cannot cross to the south of the Zadora, because the French artillery of Reille bombards them incessantly as soon as they leave the villages. The 1st division of Howard also ensures Abechuco and pursues the French withdrawal to the Zadora. At 5:00 pm. the Spaniards of Longa try to leave Durana by the south to flank the French left flank, but the artillery of the 3rd Linea prevents it; by then the troops of Reille retire to Vitoria; the other two French armies to the south also slowly retreat towards the capital. An hour later, Longa's troops will hold a brief firefight with the Franco-Spaniards fleeing to the southwest. From the beginning of the fighting on the flanks until noon, Wellington remains on the lookout, observing all the maneuvers from the heights west of Nanclares de Oca; but then his explorers inform him that the bridges over the Zadora near the town of Trespuentes remain intact and without guard. Wellington orders General Cole, of the 4th division, and Alten, of the Light Division, to cross the bridges of the Zadora River near Trespuentes.

Picton, general of the 3rd division, crosses the bridge of Mendoza without receiving any order, with a brigade of the 7th of Dalhousie; does not find resistance until positioning itself northwest of Ariñes, a key point of the French center. Towards 12:30 the allied divisions converge on the hill of Ariñez, where 2 brigades of the Army of the Center d'Erlon have a powerful battery, protected by the Leval and Darmagnac divisions to the north, and those of Villatte and Cassagne to the south. The 2nd British division of General Hill joins the attack by pressing the French from Subijana; French generals Villatte and Cassagne respond by sending two brigades against him. After bloody combats, the French d'Erlon and Gazan, pressed on all fronts by a greater number of enemies, begin to retreat in a staggered way on the road from Vitoria, to Zuazo and Gomecha. The allies harass them, but the withdrawal takes place very slowly, in good order and they can't break the cohesion of the French units, the Allied vanguards suffering some casualties. At 2:00 p.m., Cole's 4th division crosses the Zadora by the Nanclares Bridge and marches east, followed by the Portuguese cavalry of Urban. At this time all the allied troops of the center have managed to cross the Zadora, which was the first line of French defense; but they are stopped by the fire of the powerful batteries of the Ariñez hill. Towards 3:00 pm, the 7th English division attacks the town of Margarita, north of the hill of

Ariñez, and occupies it after a bloody fight, making retreat to the division of Leval, who in his flight leaves the north side of the hill vulnerable; until then his artillery had kept the allied troops away from the Zadora valley. Ahora Wellington ordena avanzar a sus divisiones contra la batería francesa del cerro. At 4:00 pm, Picton's 3rd division, supported by the 7th Division, attacked the formations north of the Ariñez hill, expelling the division of Darmargnac that defended the sector of La Hermandad, opening a gap between the troops of Gazan and d'Erlon. Picton advances behind the hill towards Zuazo, while the Alten Light Division occupies the Brotherhood. Around 4:15. Joseph reorganizes his central line and the flanks, because he fears that his armies may be involved at any time, since his men have not been able to fall back to Vitoria with the due speed and resist a strong pressure on the flanks and the center recoils to not be divided by the allied wedge. Before the front line overcomes the hill of Ariñes, the French evacuate their men and artillery. The first French central line is hurriedly organized with divisions of the Central and Southern Armies, supported by 76 pieces of artillery, and deploys from the village of Ali, in the north, to Armentia in the south. In its rear a weak second defensive line is improvised, with the troops of the Real Guard and several brigades of the Army of the Center, formed to the west of the capital. To the north, on the south bank of the Zadora, Vitoria is protected by the remains of the Army of Portugal and to the southwest, by two divisions of the Army of the South. These troops have the mission of preventing the allies in front of them from enveloping the French center. Wellington reorganizes his troops for the final offensive. Form three lines of attack with the divisions of Hill, Cole, Alten, Picton and Dalhousie. The first two lines are infantry and the last is cavalry; to the front it places almost all his artillery, about 75 cannons, to counteract the French batteries. To the north of Vitoria, in Abechuco, Gamarra and Durana, it leaves the divisions of Howard, Pack and Longa; and to the southeast, near Esquivel, leaves the Spanish regiments of the badly wounded Morillo, "El Charro", Dos Pelos and Cortazar with the brigade of the deceased Cadogan. The objective of these units is to maintain the threat of encirclement, and to press the French flanks when the main attack occurs. Around 5:00 p.m., between the towns of Ali and Armentia, a great artillery duel begins; it was the greatest of all the War of Independence. The 3rd division of Picton charges against the right flank of the French front line with the intention of flanking it, while the 2nd and 4th divisions of Hill and Cole charge for the south of Armentia, where the breach that opened an hour before their forces continues separating the divisions of d'Erlon and Gazan. Given the superiority of the allies and their compact formation of attack, at 5:30 pm General Gazan orders his divisions of the Army of the South, located in Armentia, to retire quickly on the road to Vitoria, without consulting King Joseph. The French artillerymen retreat from the first line in the same direction, towards the town of Gomecha; and the troops of the Army of the Center, in Ali, begin to retreat when being flanked by the 3ª division of Picton. At 6:00 p.m., the units of the flanks allied to the north and south of Vitoria advance, spreading among the French soldiers the rumor that they will soon be surrounded and annihilated, as their comrades on the right flank could not recover the escape route towards Bayonne; the French retreat to Vitoria all along the central line and on the flanks many begin to desert. The same Joseph retires hastily protected by his Guard that leaves the second line. The British depart from Abechuco and Gamarra crossing south of Zadora, as do the Spaniards of Longa in Durana; and the Spanish regiments descend from the hills of Puebla de Argañán; after a light gunfight, all the French on the flanks flee in panic to the east At 6:15 p.m., the cohesion of the French armies is broken and their men flee in a chaotic rout by their only possible escape route, towards Pamplona, to the east. In Gomecha they abandon much of the combat material, except the light cannon, others escape aboard a thousand carriages. King Joseph passes through Vitoria and, thanks to the protection of Reille's troops near Zurbano, arrives at

Salvatierra at 10:30; the next day he will continue his flight to Pamplona. The allies found almost all the material abandoned by the invaders on the way to Pamplona, to the town of Matauco: 151 cannons, 445 carriages with ammunition, weapons, food and other baggage, and another 1,500 carts laden with riches, many of them from King José himself. Soldiers stop pursuing the French withdrawal at 6:30 pm, stopping to loot the vehicles they find until night, finding all kinds of jewelry, expensive clothes, personal effects, artistic objects and coffers full of money: about 5.5 millions of francs.

At 7:00 pm the fighting ceases. During the day, the French had 8,000 casualties, of them 4,400 injured, 750 dead another 2,850 would be captured near the convoy, including civilians, such as the wife of General Gazan. During the following days, at least another 15,000 confused stragglers will be imprisoned. The allies suffered some 5,100 casualties, 3,660 British, 920 Portuguese and 520 Spanish. Of the total ally, some 500 British soldiers and 150 of the others would die. Wellington is upset, because he only gets about 275,000 francs, when he expected to keep all the money in cash seized. Annoyed, he will write that his men are "the scum of the earth" although this afternoon, he is the one who allows them to plunder the convoy saying: "-Leave them, they have earned their money well, and they must keep it" That will facilitate the French regrouping.

The battle of Victoria will cause the withdrawal of the Napoleonic armies from Spain. For his performance, the Marquis of Wellington will be promoted to field marshal.

22 – Spain: King Joseph Bonaparte arrives at Salvatierra during the night. General Claussel arrives at Treviño, learning that the day before José had been defeated in Vitoria. The king sent messengers, but none came to him. Go back to the southeast, to Logroño, where he had been the day before. The Site of Pamplona begins, in Navarra. South America: Manuel Belgrano enters Potosí. United States: about 2,000 British soldiers disembark on an island called Craney Island, off the coast of Virginia. The island was defended by about 150 American soldiers, but they managed to put to flight the British, who had to embark again.

23- Spain: Joseph Bonaparte arrives in Pamplona, with the remnants of the army commanded by d'Erlon, there holding a council with his generals. Many advise you to destroy the fortifications of the city and immediately continue the withdrawal to France, but the monarch decides to keep it as a meeting point for the other French armies that fall back across the peninsular northeast. He installed a garrison of 3,500 soldiers in Pamplona, entrusting the withdrawal of the French armies to the Count d'Erlon.

24- Spain: the last French garrisons leave Madrid. United States: English forces disembark in Hamton and burn it to ruins, after having perpetrated numerous murders, rapes and pillages. It appears that the perpetrators were men of the "independent foreigners companies", formed mainly by French prisoners who had agreed to join the British army, and were famous for their indiscipline. During the landing, a boat with 17 of these soldiers ran aground and its occupants were killed by the Americans despite their attempts to surrender.

25- Spain: Joseph Bonaparte leaves Pamplona at midnight and heads to Elizondo, some 15 km from the border. Wellington besieges Pamplona. The troops of Foy leave Tolosa retreating to Andoaín, exploiting the bridge after crossing the river.

26- Spain: after 06:00 in the morning Joseph Bonaparte enters France for Lesaca and Vera. The siege of San Sebastian begins, General Mendizábal positions eight battalions of Spanish soldiers in the hills of San Marcial and on the right bank of the Urumea River, cutting off the communications routes of the port city of San Sebastian; but due to the small number of its troops, it will not be able to do anything until the arrival of allied reinforcements. The city is guarded by 3,200 men under the command of the veteran General Rey; its fortifications have 58 cannons, 13 of them in a battery located on Mount Urgull and another 18 pieces in reserve. The same day of the arrival of the besiegers, the defenders destroy the neighborhoods outside the walls of San Martin and Santa Catalina, in addition to the bridge over the Urumea, and begin to fortify the convent of San Bartolommeo.

27- Vienna: the Austrian chancellor Clemens Lothar von Metternich declares that the adhesion of his country to the alliance will depend on the result of the next negotiations with Napoleon, in which it will demand the return to him of the Austrian provinces snatched in 1809. In fact, Francisco II of Austria is reluctant to join the allies in the fear that Tsar Alexander I will supplant the European hegemony of France, for which he makes an ambiguous policy of armed neutrality, in order to maintain the balance of powers. The Prussians and Russians, who agreed in June to an armistice with Bonaparte, yearn for the failure of such negotiations, because they need the Austrians to hope for victory; meanwhile they reinforce their respective armies. The British, along with the Spaniards and Portuguese, are in full offensive against the French in Spain, while, Napoleon sends more reinforcements to center-Europe to carry out a new campaign to conquest the German territories; at the moment it counts on the loyalty of the States of the Confederation of the Rhine, Baden, Bavaria, the duchy of Berg, the kingdom of Saxony, the principality of Hessen, the kingdom of Westphalia, and Wurtemberg; besides the kingdoms of Italy, Naples and the Grand Duchy of Warsaw.

28- France: Joseph Bonaparte establishes his headquarters in Saint Jean d'Luz, coastal town of the Bay of Biscay, about 5 km. of the border. The other two defeated armies in Vitoria retreat in different ways, the Portuguese, under Reille, arrives in the Baztan valley and crosses to France for Maya and Urdax, and then marches to Irun to protect the Bidasoa river frontier; the Army of the South, of the general Gazán, returns to its mother country by the steps of Roncesvalles and Valcarlos, going to Saint Jean du Pied d'Port to protect the French southern border. The last contingents that still remain in Spain are the Army of the North, some 15,000 men under Claussel, and the divisions of Generals Foy and Palombini, who would number another 16,000 soldiers, and Suchet's army of some 15,000 soldiers, Valencia and the south of Catalonia.

This is how, three weeks after the battle of Vitoria some 70,000 French soldiers are withdrawn from Spain, Napoleon will destine them to protect the southern border of France; another 7,000 are besieged in Pamplona, San Sebastian and Zaragoza. The Marquis of Wellington currently concentrates about 100,000 allied soldiers in the area of northwestern Spain, plus the 8,000 guerrillas of Espoz and Mina. The last French force in Spain is the Army of the South of Suchet, with 15,000 soldiers distributed in garrisons around the river Jucar, in Valencia. When Suchet was informed of the Allied advance towards the northeast, he began to gather his men, retreating to the north, harassed by the guerrillas of "El Fraile" until taking refuge in Tarragona.

29- Spain: conquest of Forts of Pancorbo. After being defeated the French armies in Vitoria, there is only a garrison of 700 isolated French in Spanish territory, stationed in the forts of Santa Maria and Santa Engracia de Pancorbo, which rise on steep hills, guarding both sides of the gorge in the road from Burgos to Vitoria. General O'Donell, of the Andalusia Army, marched with several thousand soldiers to recover them; taking the fort of Santa Maria, the smaller of the two, during the afternoon. Then he placed, at night and with the help of sappers, a battery at the top of the hill of Cimera. The French try to prevent it by firing their artillery and rifles, but the Spaniards raise the cannons and open fire on the fortress that night.

30- Spain: Pancorbo forts. When the Hispanics were about to storm the fort of Santa Engracia, their commander decided to surrender. At that time the last French armies retreat towards France, leaving small garrisons in Pamplona, Zaragoza and San Sebastian; there is no one left south of the Ebro River.

JULY-1813

1- France: dismissal of Joseph Bonaparte. Napoleon blames his brother and Marshal Jourdan for the defeat suffered in Vitoria and the subsequent withdrawal from Spain. In Dresden, today he signs a decree by which he removes them from any military command and names Marshal Soult in his place as Lieutenant General of the Spanish Army, with the mission of occupying the north of the Ebro River and defending the southern French border. The frustrated Joseph Bonaparte will continue to retain the Spanish crown nominally, as he will be living in France in his palace of Mortefontaine, separated with his Council of Ministers from any relevant political decision. Although Napoleon appointed him Lieutenant of the Kingdom, he will disappear practically from the public scene, until next year his brother will entrust him with the military defense of Paris.

2- United States: 600 soldiers leave the Fort George with the mission to capture Beaver Dams, defended by fifty British and some 400 Indians, but the expedition will be a complete disaster, as it ended with about 100 Americans killed and the rest taken prisoner. The Americans retained Fort George, but they will no longer attempt other incursions into Canada. South America: Simon Bolívar obtains the victory in the battle of Niquitao.

3 – England: Arthur Wellesley, Marquis of Wellington, is promoted to Marshal.

4- United States: a large group of Creek Indians, led by Chief Peter McQueen, went to Spanish Florida to buy ammunition with a letter signed by a British officer. Having learned of this operation, the Americans sent a party of soldiers from Fort Mims to seize the cargo. They were surprised at Burnt Corn Creek while they were sleeping tonight, attacked them and fled towards the swamps. When the soldiers were engaged in looting Indian possessions, the creeks counterattacked and dispersed the Americans. The Creeks assumed that the American attack was a declaration of war.

5 – Spain: British troops landing in Alicante.

6- South America: in Chile, José Miguel Carrera put under siege the city of Chillan, where the royalist troops had concentrated to spend the winter.

7- Río de la Plata: José Caparrós, a Spanish lieutenant settled in Uruguay and newly appointed by the patriots commander of the town of Viboras, assaults the royalist armory of the island of Martin Garcia, taking with him some of the armament and ammunition, for which he is promoted to captain.

8- South America: sent by Toribio Montes to regain control of the southern viceroyalty, Colonel Juan de Samano occupies the position of governor of the disputed Popayan, in Colombia, where he proclaims the Constitution of Cadiz, is promoted to brigadier and intimate to the rebels of Cundinamarca to take an oath of obedience to Spain.

9- Spain, siege of San Sebastian: the British general Graham at the head of the British 5th division, a German brigade, another Portuguese, and heavy artillery, reaching the allies now a total of 10,000 men. The engineers determine that the eastern side of the fortress, the Zurriola wall, is the weakest, and install batteries in a parallel line, bombarding the wall, also attack with incendiary rockets the convent of San Bartolommeo.

72

11- North America: this morning the expedition of Mauricio Arze and Lagos Garcia returns to New Mexico, departing from Abiquiu in March of this year to the Lake of the Tympanogos, in Utah, to trade with the Utes Timpanogos (which is prohibited from 1778), when the Spaniards refused to buy them slaves, the Indians killed 8 of their horses and one mule. The Spaniards fled to the river of Santa Isabel where they found other Indians who guided them to the bearded Utes (because strangely they have beards), who received them well but also tried to kill them when the Spaniards refused to buy them slaves, so they marched to the Rio Grande (today Colorado), where they arrived at the village of Guasache, where they agreed to buy 12 slaves to avoid problems and after losing two more chivalry crossing this river, they started back with only 109 purchased skins.

12- France: Soult takes command of the armies that escaped from the Peninsula, and with its troops organizes the new Spanish Army, with four corps of three divisions each.

15- Spain, siege of Pamplona: the English are relieved by the Army of Andalusia, some 15,000 Spanish soldiers of General O'Donnell, who are limited to encircle the city, for lack of the artillery that is being used by Wellington on the border and the Siege of San Sebastian. At the beginning of August, other regiments of the Army of Galicia will arrive.

16- South America: the United Provinces of New Granada (Colombia) proclaim their absolute independence and become a republic: Nariño is appointed head of the joint revolutionary forces of the United Provinces and Cundinamarca.

17- Spain, San Sebastian: the defenders leave the convent, which is ruined by fires and landslides; the British find about 250 dead soldiers inside. The besieged go on to harass the Allies' trenches and their batteries from a redoubt; conquered by the English in another assault shortly after.

20- South America: when attacking in the middle of winter, the Chileans of the dictator José Miguel Carrera are defeated in the siege of Chillan by the army sent by the Viceroy of Peru under the command of Juan Francisco Sanchez, who defends the city.

21- South America: in Venezuela Bolívar defeats the royalist commander Francisco Oberto in the battle of Los Horcones.

22- Spain, San Sebastian: the besiegers, after firing with ten 24-pounder guns for 15 and a half hours at some 3,500 bullets, bombs and grenades, manage to open a gap of up to 50 meters in the wall of Zurriola, and another 10 meters after demolish part of a tower and the adjacent bastion of San Telmo.

24- Spain: Soult returns to invade the country by Roncesvalles, with the aim of helping the French garrison besieged in Pamplona; d'Erlon covers his right flank entering the Batzan. They fight with the allied soldiers that defend the zones, corresponding to the center and the right of the Allied deployment, the first ones retreat to Irurita, and the others to Lizozín and Zubiri, although the León regiment defends the munitions factory of Orbaiceta until he is forced to retreat.

25 – Spain, first assault on San Sebastian: Graham, urged by Wellington, ordered a triple attack at low tide with the aim of climbing the wall of San Carlos and to assault the two gaps in the walls, sending first two contingents to follow reinforcement. The French, attentive to the maneuver, let the British approach, firing cannon shots and rifle shots when they are nearby, causing them to retreat in disarray, slipping with the tangle of algae and polished rocks from the shore of the sea and the Urumea River creating a great confusion and panic, they suffered about 2,000 casualties; the defenders had less than 70 dead. Graham calls for a ceasefire to pick up his wounded before the tide rises and drown, General Rey grants it. For its part, the advance of Soult is so fast, that one of its outposts almost captured the same Wellington when he was making a reconnaissance with a small escort, near San Sebastian.

26- Spain, San Sebastian: Wellington ordered the suspension of the attacks to have more heavy artillery, which will be brought from England by the Royal Navy and part to East with several units, to repel an incursion that General Soult makes in the area of the Pyrenees. The siege continues, but for the moment the hostilities cease. The allies are still retreating to the south, avoiding more engagements due to the numerical superiority of Soult in its penetration zone, the Alduides valley.

27- Spain: Wellington forms a line of contention north of Pamplona, the French objective. O'Donell, who is besieging the capital, sends reinforcements to the front, leaving the regiments of Carlos of Spain in the siege. In total, some 12,000 allies are deployed in front of Huarte and in the hills of Villalba covering Pamplona. The Right Corp, commanded by Reille, the Center, d'Erlon, and the Claussel Left, and the Reserve, under the command of Villatte. They were supported by a Cavalry Corps with three divisions, two heavy cavalries under the command of Tilly and Treilhard, and another of light cavalry, commanded by Soult; in total they would add about 60,000 soldiers; In addition, Suchet groups to the south of Catalonia another 15,000 men. While the French were reorganizing Wellington has had time to deploy more troops in the border sector of the Vascongadas and Navarra, west of the Pyrenees, where the French are concentrated, but however Wellington cannot count on all its strength, being several Allied units surrounding Pamplona and San Sebastian, where the French left garrisons in their retreat. To the east, on the right wing, the Port of Roncesvalles holds the Spanish division of Morillo, the brigade of Wing and the 4th division of Cole, in Viscarret. In the center, in the valleys of Batzan and Alduides, are the 2nd division of Hill, the Portuguese of Amarante and Campbell. In the left wing, to the northwest, in Santa Bárbara, Vera and Echelar, there are the Light Division of Alten and the 7th of Dalhausie. Wellington leaves in rearguard like reserves to the 6ª division of Pack, to 3ª of Picton and the Hispanic one of Longa, these two in Olagüe. In this border strip there will be about 36,000 soldiers, in the northeastern part of Spain there are nearly 100,000 allies, to which the troops of the guerrilla parties would have to be added. Soult arrives with about 25,000 soldiers to the mountains between Ostiz and Zubiri, attacking south towards Pamplona; the besieged garrison collaborates making an exit in the same sense of the assault. The Spanish regiments of Moreda and Llanas, with the help of one Portuguese and another British, block the offensive by defending a strategic hill on the Soult route; even so the French manage to arrive until Souraren, to a few kilometers of the north of the besieged capital. North America: the creek Indians (red sticks) had obtained gunpowder and ammunition from the Spanish governor of Pensacola (Florida), delivered for the hunt in a gesture of goodwill, but with this reinforcement they defeated the Americans at the Battle of Burnt Corn (Arroyo of Alabama) and cause the massacre of Fort Mims, which will provoke claims by the US government against Spain, which had pledged not to arm the Indian tribes.

28- Spain: the French attack again the line of Wellington, tried to flank it by his left, being rejected after a fierce fight, which cost 3,000 casualties in exchange for 2,600 allies, mostly British. Soult, anticipating that he could not cross it, decides to send the heavy artillery back to France with his ammunition and equipment, accompanied by several hundred wagons transporting the wounded.

29- Spain: the division of Hill arrives from the northeast to reinforce the allied line of Pamplona, threatening the rearguard of the French right flank by Marcalaín. Soult desists to break the siege of the capital, opting for his second objective, to help the also besieged garrison of San Sebastian, trying to pass through the south of Marcalaín, attacking the left of the Wellington line while the Center Corps of D ' Erlon would press Hill's troops.

30- Spain: in the morning Wellington understands Soult's maneuver and cuts him off with a direct counterattack, producing another bloody combat that results in 2,000 French casualties and 1,900 British casualties. Next, Wellington sends reinforcements to his left flank to make his way to Hill's positions and reinforce him; the pressure of Count d'Erlon had driven him back to the north of Marcaláin. South America: applying the decree of the Cortes de Cadiz that suppressed the courts of the Inquisition, Viceroy Abascal suppresses the Court of Lima, the population loots and destroys belongings and part of the archives.

31 – Spain: combat of Venta de Urroz. South America: Bolivar defeats the Spanish Colonel Julian Izquierdo at the Battle of Taguanes.

AUGUST-1813

1- Spain: combats in Sumbilla and Yanzi. Mexico: José Alvarez de Toledo displaces Bernardo Gutierrez de Lara and is recognized as president of Texas.

2- Spain: the decided British attack pushes Soult's armies northwards, retreating through the same terrain for which he had advanced days before, crosses the border again, after having 5,000 dead and wounded, another 3,000 are taken prisoner; the allies suffered about 4,500 casualties. The fighting during the Allied counterattack amounts to total French casualties to 10,000 and allies to about 7,000. This battle marks the beginning of the allied offensive towards the south of France.

3- United States: After its defeat in Fort Meigs, Procter tried to seize of a base of provisions located in Fort Stephenson. He began to deploy his artillery, but, considering that Harrison could go and break the siege, he decided to launch an attack this day. It had 1,400 men between British and Indians, while in the fort there were about 160 American soldiers under the command of George Croghan, who managed to repel one assault after another until the enemy retired.

4- South America: in Chile, the siege of Chillan was weakening due to continuous defections, for that reason José Miguel Carrera decided to launch an attack before it was too late. The maneuvers began that same night, the Chileans managed to enter the city, but they were dispersed and put to flight by the royalists. Finally, a cannonball hit a piece of Chilean artillery causing an explosion that spread to several nearby gunpowder deposits. The Chileans had many casualties and soon abandoned the fight.

5- Spain: the governor of Zaragoza decides to capitulate. South America: Bolívar defeats General Montverde in Puerto Cabello.

6- South America: Simon Bolívar triumphantly enters Caracas, where he will organize the Second Republic of Venezuela. With it ended a successful military campaign that received the name of admirable campaign.

7- The Treaty of Bucharest between Russia and the Ottoman Empire stipulated the withdrawal of Russia from Serbian territory, although the Turks undertook to respect the independence of Serbia (which remained a province of the Empire). However, seeing Russia focused on European politics, the Turks invaded the territory simultaneously by three places. Karagjorgje fled to Hungary shortly after, and there he was captured and imprisoned by the Austrians.

8- Mexico: Acapulco surrender to Mexican insurgents.

10- South America: Carrera, with his army reduced by casualties and desertions, leaves the site of Chillan and retires to Concepcion.

12 - Austria declares war on France. After the failure of the peace negotiations with the French, the Austrian emperor today decides to position himself definitively on the side of the coalition: England, Prussia, Russia and Sweden. For the Germans, this is the Second War of Liberation. The Prussian and Russian armies advance from Breslau, with the aim of falling on the flank of the French troops, stationed next to the Bohemian mountains, to close the road to Saxony for the Elbe valley, while the Austrians cross the mountainous passages of Bohemia. The allies mobilize a formidable armed contingent of 405,000 soldiers, of which 150,000 are Russians, 115,000 Austrians, 75,000 Prussians and 19,000 Swedes, the rest belong to other nationalities, such as Poles, Germans or English. Between all they displace an imposing artillery park of about 1,400 pieces. Bernadotte, Prince of Sweden and former marshal of Napoleon, directs the Swedish North Army, 130,000 Russians, Prussians and Swedes with about 300 cannons, located between Berlin and Sttetin. The British who serve among the Swedes provide rockets for military use. Blücher and Wittgenstein command the Prussian Army of Silesia, of 62,000 Prussians and Russians, with about 300 cannons in Breslau, where the Army of Poland will meet, with some 33,000 Russians with 120 cannons, commanded by Bennigsen. Marshal Schwarzemberg, leading the Austrian Bohemian Army, of 115,000 Austrians with 380 cannons and 65,000 Russians with 300 cannons, will be the commander-in-chief of the allied armies. Barclay de Tolly is the leader of all the Russian forces, divided among the aforementioned armies. Meanwhile, in Spain, the English, Spanish and Portuguese are approaching the southern border of France after defeating the troops of King Joseph in Vitoria. With Austria in the Coalition, the balance of forces in Europe definitely leans against Napoleon, counting his enemies with more troops and resources than he does; the 10-week truce has benefited them and the situation of the French becomes very compromised; at the moment the allies outnumber them in artillery. Napoleon will have in total, with reinforcements on the way, with 300,000 soldiers in the vicinity of Bautzen and another 100,000 deployed on the west bank of the Elbe. The French and their allies total 333,000 infantrymen, 26,000 artillerymen with 775 cannons and some 41,000 horsemen. The presence of the emperor in the campaign has raised the morale. The French army is organized into 14 Army Corps; the 1st in command of Vandamme, the 2nd of Victor, the 3rd of Ney, the 4th of Bertrand, the 5th of Lauriston, the 6th of Marmont, the 7th of Reynier, the 8th of Poniatowsky, the 9th of Augerau, the 10th of Rapp, the 11th of MacDonald, the 12th of Oudinot, the 13th of Davout, and the 14th of Saint Cyr. In addition, they are accompanied by 5 Cavalry Corps, 1st by Lateur Maubourg, 2nd by Sebastini, 3rd by Arreghi, 4th by Sokolnicki and 5th by Pajol; and the troops of the Imperial Guard, among them the division of the Old Guard, five of Young Guard, one of artillery, with some 200 pieces, and another of cavalry, all under the command of Mortier. Of the total, some 160,000 are French. The others belong to other allied states, among them 12,000 Poles, 9,000 Italians, 6,000 Saxons, 5,000 Badens, 3,500 Westerners, 2,500 Hessians and 2,000 Westphalians. The rest come from the Confederation of the Rhine, apart from the Bavarians or the Duchy of Berg. In addition to this maneuvering mass, Bonaparte maintains a special corps commanded by General Girard, with two infantry divisions, an artillery reserve, a unit of engineers and a detachment of observation before Leipzig, in short about 30,000 soldiers. The current state of La Grande Armée, made up of very young and inexperienced recruits, will be criticized by Napoleon himself, who will write in those days: "We are giving you 8 ounces of bread, 3 of rice and 8 of meat." Which is not enough in his opinion, because as he said once: "- An army marches to the rhythm of his stomach ..." And at least 100,000 of his men are undernourished.

14- United States: the American ship Argus was dedicated to capture commercial boats in British territorial waters, but this morning it was sighted by the Pelican, who, after three quarters of an hour of bombing was in a position to approach it, but then the Argus surrendered.

15 - Germany: the Grande Armée begins to maneuver. Bonaparte orders his troops to retire from the vicinity of the Bohemian gorges, where the Austrians will arrive, and positions them around Grlitz and Bautzen, while the 13th Corps of Marshal Davout protects the maneuver. His soldiers occupy positions in the Elbe, Pirna, Koningstein and the fortifications of Dresden, crucial for the French deployment. The engineers build a fortified belt around the capital and a solid bridge on the right bank of the Elbe. Bonaparte plans to defend the course line of the Elbe River by using it as a rear guard. Start your campaign crossing the river with the Grande Armée by the bridge, your main objective is Berlin, which calculates to 4 or 5 days away. The secondary objective will be to help the French garrisons of Kstrin, Stettin and Spandau.

16- Mexico: Mariano Matamoros defeats the battalion of Asturias under the command of Manuel Martinez and Juan Candano in the second battle of San Agustin del Palmar.

17 – Spain: Suchet's troops leave Tarragona and retire to France. Mexico: The Royalists of Texas initiate a counterattack against the rebels deprived support of the American mercenaries, are defeated in the battle of Medina. José Álvarez de Toledo had about 1,400 men, of whom only a hundred survived after four hours of fighting. The royalists, under the command of José Joaquin de Arredondo, counted 55 casualties. After this victory, Arredondo dedicated himself to expurgate Texas of rebels. Alvarez de Toledo fled to the United States. In San Antonio, the Spaniards executed some 300 people.

18- Germany: Napoleon decides to wait for some days impatiently hoping to guess the strategy of the allies.

19 – Spain: combat of Amposta. South America: Santiago Mariño enters the Venezuelan city of Barcelona.

20- Germany: Napoleon finally decides to continue with his initial plan to advance on Berlin, to put out of combat the Prussians. To this end, it sends several of its Army Corps to the capital, a total of some 130,000 soldiers. Blucher, commander of the Silesian Army, protects the road to Berlin with 80,000 Prussians and Russians, among whom there are several units of Bennigsen's Polish Army. When informed that Napoleon has started the campaign, he opts to retire to the eastern bank of the Haynau River, to make the invaders persecute him and be able to face them in more favorable terrain. North America: 1,400 rebels led by the Cuban José Alvarez de Toledo and Dubois and supported by the Apaches, are completely defeated at the Battle of Medina, 20 miles south of San Antonio, the bloodiest fought on Texas soil, by the commander general Joaquin de Arredondo commanded 1,830 men (including Lieutenant Antonio Lopez de Santa Anna, who will try to emulate him 23 years later), shortly after take San Antonio, where they proclaim Cristobal Dominguez as governor of Texas. Less than 100 Republicans manage to flee the battlefield and their 1,300 dead are hung from the trees and left in place for 9 years. The Spanish authorities destroy the rebellious Texan population of Trinidad.

21 - Germany, Löwenberg combat: this morning the French vanguard reaches the enemy's rearguard near Löwenberg, causing the allies some 2,000 casualties. In the afternoon another fight is fought on the Katzbach River. However, Schwarzenberg moves towards the Elbe Valley with a larger contingent than Bonaparte expected, so he leaves the 11th MacDonald Corps in front of Blucher and retreats with the other Corps towards Bautzen, with the intention of crossing the mountains of Bohemia and attack the Austrians in Kdnigstein.

22- Germany: first combat in Pirna; Wittgenstein defeats Saint Cyr's troops. Blücher, commanding the Silesian Army, with about 80,000 Prussian and Russian soldiers, retired after holding a first confrontation with superior troops in number of the Grande Armée, forming a new line on the banks of the River Haynau on August 25, maneuvering today on the course of the Katzbach River. Spain: Wellington returns to the siege of San Sebastian with more troops and artillery brought from the United Kingdom.

23- Germany, battle of Grossbeeren: to conquer the capital of Prussia and eliminate them from the war, Napoleon sends Marshal Oudinot to the command of the Berlin Army, consisting of the 4th, 7th and 12th Army Corps and a Cavalry Corps of the Grande Armée; In total there are 70,000 infants, 4,000 horsemen and 216 cannons. Bonaparte orders to destroy Berlin if he opposes resistance; the Prince of Sweden, Bernadotte, is the only one who could prevent it, commanding 98,000 Prussians, Swedes and Russians. Troops of the 7th Corps of Reynier occupy the city of Grossbeeren, just 10 miles south of Berlin, when the Prussians led by Von Bulow launch a determined attack and expel them with some ease, as many French are inexperienced recruits. A dense rain hinders action and contributes to confusion. The French divisions of Guilleume and Fournier counterattack, dislodge the allies and conquest Grossbeeren at cost of 1,500 casualties, but Oudinot does not react quickly enough, allowing the Allies to regroup suffering scarce losses; after noticing the situation the marshal orders hastily retired. At around 8:00 p.m., a French rear column meets a Prussian Hussar unit and a cavalry fight takes place until the darkness of the night stops the fight. Throughout the night the French continue to retreat and lose more men in sporadic clashes. The French suffer 3,000 casualties among the dead, wounded and prisoners, in addition to losing about 13 cannons; the allies have about 1,000 casualties. For the Prussians this battle is their first victory since 1806 and raises their morale to a great extent.

25- Germany: the vanguard of the Armies of Bohemia and Reserve, with 80,000 Austrians, Prussians and Russians, appears before the city of Dresden, capital of the Kingdom of Saxony and one of the key points of the French deployment. The city was garrisoned by two brigades, which are joined by the 14th Army Corps commanded by Saint Cyr, in total will add about 20,000 soldiers. The city is precariously protected by a defensive line of 8 km of batteries, redoubts and barricades, making it impossible for its defenders to resist for a long time an assault of such magnitude. The allies stop to celebrate a Council of War, as Tsar Alexander I of Russia, Emperor Franz II of Austria, and King William III of Prussia have different political objectives in their common campaign against the French Empire, and must stand agreement on the action to be taken, despite the opinion of the supposed allied commander-in-chief, Prince Karl Von Schwarzenberg.

26- Germany, Battle of Katzbach: Napoleon sends MacDonald's 11th Army Corps to Katzbach, but the Prussians quickly counterattack, forcing the French to retreat. Bonaparte sends more reinforcements; first comes the division of General Souham; but Blücher orders another attack, causing great losses; the French concentrate in the area up to 130,000 men; which does not prevent them from suffering 15,000 casualties among the dead and wounded, losing 100 cannons. Spain, San Sebastian: the allies have already placed 67 pieces of artillery: 9 howitzers, 16 mortars, 32 heavy cannons and 6 others lighter; distributed in eight batteries. They open fire simultaneously against the sides of the breaches, enlarging them, and against several bastions, disabling all their artillery. Four days later, the walls and houses that were in a strip of 250 meters have been completely razed.

27 - Germany, battle of Dresden: Napoleon abandons his plan to attack the Austrians in Kdnigstein. Leaving Vandamme's 1st Corps in the mountains of Bohemia, he ordered the Great Armée to retreat in aid of the threatened Saxon capital, forcing one of the most spectacular marches in military history, traveling its army 90 miles in 72 hours, reaching Dresden this dawn. At 05:00 hours, a few hours after the first French reinforcement troops entered the city, the allies begin their attack. The Prussians advance through the Royal Gardens, defeating the defenders who are on their way, until they hear the distant shouts of joy from the defenders of:

"- Long live the Emperor ... !!" at the moment when Napoleon enters Dresden with his Guard. Tsar Alexander and Emperor Francisco intend to desist when they learn that Bonaparte is in the city, but King Guillermo persuades them to continue the fight. During the morning there are several allied attacks, lacking in coordination, tenaciously repelled by the defenders, to which more Army Corps of the Grande Armée are added; even so, after five hours of fighting the French of Saint Cyr are exhausted, they have lost ground and new allied troops are approaching the capital. When Schwarzenberg prepares to launch a final assault and enter Dresden, Napoleon orders the 70,000 soldiers of the 2nd Corps of Victor, the 6th of Marmont and the 14th of Saint Cyr to counterattack supported by the 1st and 5th Corps of Cavalry, sending your own Guard to fight. Then there is a stubborn fight that lasts for the rest of the morning and afternoon, the French push back the allies despite their greater number. At night a torrential rain begins to fall and the hostilities are interrupted; the allies are demoralized because they have not managed to gain ground. During the night they receive reinforcements, until adding about 170,000 men, almost half Austrians, and 488 cannons. The French also receive reinforcements of infantry and cavalry, reaching 158,000 men and about 450 pieces of artillery.

28- Germany, battle of Dresden: At daybreak Bonaparte deploys 90,000 of his men in the center to contain the allies, while attacking with the remaining 35,000 on each flank, the left under the command of Mortier, with two divisions of the Young Guard, and those on the right in command de Murat, with Veteran Line Infantry. At 06:00 hours, the French begin their pincer maneuver against the Allied flanks, causing serious losses to the enemy, who nevertheless defends their positions until shortly before 12:00 when they retreat in the whole line, although in good order. At around 3:00 p.m., the 2nd Prussian Corps of Von Kleist and the Austrian divisions of Marshal Gyulai, on the Allied left flank, are completely overwhelmed and pushed to the east by Murat's troops, suffering some 24,000 casualties. Meanwhile, Generals Wittgenstein and von Hessen Homburg, on the Allied right flank, are overtaken and enveloped by Mortier, who captures many of his infantry; through the center the French advance. The confrontations conclude around 4:00 pm, when the Bohemian Army, now without flanks, begins to retreat, defeated; the last clashes will take place at nightfall. The allies lose 15,000 captured men and 23,000 wounded or dead, and lose about 40 cannons. The French have 10,000 casualties among wounded and dead, including General Jean Moreau. Napoleon seems discouraged, at night he is seen shivering in the heat of a bonfire in the camp, absorbed in his thoughts. It seems to have lost the impetus of yesteryear; he does not even give instructions regarding the immediate pursuit of the Allied retreat, as would be usual; this victory will be the last great triumph of his career. In Dresden the 14th Corps of Saint Cyr will remain stationed, with some 25,000 soldiers, and will no longer participate in the rest of the campaign, like Davout, destined to garrison Hamburg with 30,000 soldiers. In total, the Grande Armée will dedicate up to 80,000 men to garrison German cities and fortresses, which according to many French generals is a grave mistake. This battle is the second of the Napoleonic Wars in number of fighters.

29- Germany, combat of Leitskau: Hirschberg defeats the French of Giraud. Second Combat of Pirna, Württemberg defeats Vandamme's troops. Battles of Priesten and Kulm: Napoleon orders Marshal Vandamme, commanding the 1st French Army Corps, and other reinforcement units, about 37,000 soldiers stationed in southern Saxony, which harass the march of the Bohemian Army, retreating after being defeated in Dresden. The Austrian troops of Schwarzenberg retreat on mountain paths and gorges to their homeland, followed by the Prussians of Blücher and the Russians of Barclay de Tolly. Bonaparte plans to intercept the enemies in Kulm and Teplitz, where the 1st Corps must resist waiting for the divisions of

Marshal Mortier's Young Guard, then the 6th and 14th Corps would arrive in the west and surround the allies. United States: the creek Indians of Peter McQueen attack Fort Mims by surprise. McQueen made an alliance with another creek chief named William Weatherford. These Indians had such "un-Indian" names because their parents were British. The Creeks had participated in a project conceived by Washington and continued by Jefferson of cultural assimilation of the Indians. Some of these half-Indians had become fully integrated into American society, as was the case of Captain Dixon Bailey, who was one of the senior officers at Fort Mims and a personal enemy of Weatherford. Some Creeks Indians also lived in the fort as refugees because of the civil war that shook their tribe. Almost a thousand warriors managed to take the fort, and then killed and tore the hair of almost all of its inhabitants, in what is known as the Fort Mims massacre. Only 36 people were able to escape, including Bailey, although mortally wounded. The Indians spared the lives of the black slaves in the fort, whom they kept as slaves. This event spread panic among the American settlers in the area, who began to mobilize to wage a war against the Indians, the Creek War.

30- Germany: At 06:00 hours, the French assault Priesten from the north, expelling the Russians from the Prince of Wittenberg after a bloody battle. At noon they attack the Austrians quartered in Kulm, also dislodging them, causing the allies a total of 6,000 casualties, the French lose an equal number, but their morale is very high. Vandamme occupies the small mountainous valley, placing its divisions on a defensive line southwest of Kulm, to cut off the flight route of the Bohemian Army. However, the Mortier Corps, Saint Cyr and Marmont are behind in allowing the allies to regroup; Vandamme expects reinforcements that will not arrive. The Russian general Ostermann-Tolstoy concentrates to the 5º of Guards, 3º of Grenadiers and the 1º and 2º Russian Corps to the southwest of Kulm, adding about 44,000 soldiers. Tolstoy knows of the distance of the other French forces, and decides to make a frontal attack immediately, taking advantage of his momentary numerical superiority. The allies begin their advance through their center, while the French counter-attack on the Allied left flank. At that time two Austrian divisions arrive in the valley and join the attack, but the determined defenders reject them and force them to retreat towards Toplice. In the afternoon the remains of the 2nd Prussian Corps commanded by Von Kleist arrive in the northeast of Kulm, about 10,000 soldiers fleeing the 14th Corps of Saint Cyr, anxious to avenge the massacre of their unit in Dresden. The allies total about 70,000 men, more than double what the French count. The Austrians advance with redoubled spirit and begin to surround the French left, because the Prussian threat behind their back frightens its inexperienced soldiers, practically surrounded by a larger army, because the reinforcements promised by Napoleon do not arrive; Vandamme diverts troops from the center to his rear. The Russians take Priesten, while the French left retreats. Vandamme desperately orders his divisions to retreat northward and break through the Prussians to escape the encirclement; Many units lose discipline because of fear and flee in disarray. The Prussians of Kleist turn away from the avalanche of French followed by Russians and Austrians. The rest of the fighting takes place in this chaos, until the French survivors disperse. Vandamme himself is wounded and captured by a Cossack unit, 7,000 of his men are apprehended and another 6,000 are wounded or killed. The allies capture 82 cannons, 2 banners and 5 flags; but they have suffered about 11,000 casualties. The Bohemian Army can withdraw to Austria and reorganize, thanks to this tactical victory. Tsar Alexander will accuse Vandamme of banditry, but stocking up on the ground was a common practice in armies when they run out of supplies they carry. Napoleon will blame Vandamme for this disaster, which he considers dead, but the truth is that it was his other Army Corps that could not help him as he had planned. It is one of the worst defeats of all his campaigns. South America: Bolivar defeats Montverde again in Barbula, farm neighboring the town of Naguanagua; Venezuela.

31- Spain: second assault on San Sebastian, at 11:00 in the morning, several columns of British soldiers jump from the trenches of the beach and attack the breach of the bastion of San Juan, fighting a bloody combat with the French that awaited them there. To the brief, the Portuguese brigade leaves its posts, fords the Urumea River and unfolds in two columns attacks by the great breach of the wall of Zurriola, also found great resistance; meanwhile, the Allied artillery continues to beat other points of the fortifications. After 2:00 pm, the defenders continue to reject the allies when a projectile reaches a powder keg, causing a large number of casualties among the garrison. Anglo-Portuguese take advantage of the bewilderment, regroup and organize another assault quickly, entering the city, but the French withdraw in order to the Castillo de la Mota and the fortified convent of Santa Teresa, leaving behind some 280 wounded. The civilian population exults with joy at the streets, balconies and windows to receive the victors with shouts of joy, but the British and Portuguese soldiers shoot them, then devote themselves to looting, killing those who try to prevent the rape of their wives and daughters ; actions consented by the officers. Some soldiers arrive from the camps and even from the ships anchored nearby, without arms and with mules, to carry all the possible booty; At dusk the capital of San Sebastian is on fire. During the siege of the city, the French garrison of General Rey has suffered more than 2,000 casualties, but still remains locked in the Castillo de la Mota. The allies will have had some 3,200 casualties; among them the engineer Richard Fletcher, who designed the fortifications of the Torres Vedras Line; and Generals Leith, Oswald and Robinson are wounded.

Battle of San Marcial: after the failure of Soult's troops in their attempt to rescue the garrison of San Sebastian, some 9,000 French soldiers from the divisions of Maucune and Lamartiere, commanded by General Reille, cross this morning to the south bank of the Bidasoa river near Hendaya, with the objective of helping their encircled companions, who await an allied attack imminently. Protecting the right flank of the Anglo-Portuguese of the Marquis of Wellington, who will attack the capital within a few hours, the 3rd, 5th and 7th divisions of the 4th Spanish Army are deployed, stationed in the line of hills and hills of the town of San Marcial. Behind them are two brigades of the 4th division and the Spanish division of Longa. At 08:00 hours, the French attack the Spanish outposts and advance towards the south, arriving at the town of Soroya, where they are rejected by the heavy fusillade discharges of the Asturias regiment. Reille retreats and builds a bridge to the west, near Las Nasas, sheltered by batteries located north of the Bidasoa, which keep the Spanish vanguard away. The French divisions cross the bridge and attack the center of the Spanish line, being thrown down hills by troops of General Porlier's division and a Navy battalion, retaining only Mount Irechaval. Reille regroups his men and leads another attack against the Hispanic left, defended by a brigade of the 3rd division of General Ezpeleta, which under the pressure of the attack retreats in order, while the attackers take their camp. General Mendizabal, commander of all the units in the sector, goes with the division of Porlier and, ordering furious charges to the bayonet manages to expel the French from all the positions they had conquered, forcing them to retreat over the bridge and the fords at nightfall under a torrential rain. The French suffered some 3,600 casualties, and the Spaniards, some 2,600; while this battle was being fought, the English and Portuguese allies entered San Sebastian. This has been the last great confrontation on Spanish soil during the War of Independence; henceforth the great fighting will be waged in territories of France.

SEPTEMBER-1813

1- Spain: combat of Vera. Before the advance of the Allied armies, the 10,000 soldiers of General Vandamme retreat to the north of the Bidasoa in the direction of France, having to make their way over the bridge of Vera, guarded by a detachment of the 95th British regiment, about 70 Englishmen under the command of the captain Cadoux Under cover, occupying the abrupt high positions that surround the area, they keep the French at a distance shooting during the whole day, without receiving reinforcements, until their ammunition is exhausted, retiring at nightfall. Only then did Vandamme's troops dare to cross the bridge, abandoning their artillery and baggage.

2- Mexico: Ignacio Elizondo, whose treachery made it possible to capture the Mexican insurgent leaders in 1811, is recognized by Lieutenant Miguel Serrano, who assassinates him with knife slashes while sleeping in his camp on the San Marcos River, Texas.

3- South America: when Bolívar was besieging Puerto Cabello, in Venezuela, the royalist leader Antonio Zuazola is captured by the patriots and hanged.

4- Río de la Plata: the ship "San Pablo", the frigate "Puebla" and the brig "San José" arrive in Montevideo from Cadiz, escorting 4 merchants, with 2,200 soldiers and war supplies.

5- United States: the American battleship Enterprise sighted near the coasts of the State of Maine the British Boxer, and both were prepared for combat. After half an hour, the Boxer was broken. The British captain, Samuel Blythe, died just after the battle, and the American, William Burrows, mortally wounded, refused to accept Blythe's sword as a sign of surrender, ordering that it be sent to the family of the deceased. His last words were: I'm satisfied, I'm happy.

8 – Spain, end of the San Sebastian Site. When the allies successfully raided the walls of the city on August 31, the French garrison commanded by General Rey retreated to the citadel of Castillo de la Mota, continuing its desperate and tenacious resistance here. The British of General Graham moved 59 pieces of artillery, among which there are only 17 heavy cannons, the other mortars and howitzers, distributed in three batteries. At 09:00 today, the British open fire with all their cannons, collapsing the walls of the Mirador and the battery of the Queen until a projectile hits the powder keg of the defenders exploding all their ammunition with a great crash. Unable to continue the defense, General Rey capitulates and sends a colonel with a white flag to parley. General Graham receives him courteously, saying: "... after the brilliant defense your troops have made, they cannot be considered defeated and have the right to dictate conditions ..." At sunset, 1,850 Frenchmen parade outside the castle, 481 of them sick or wounded, with their banners deployed, in front of the allies in formation; General Rey and his men are taken prisoner. However, the morale of the English is very low because of the delay in payments, and they refuse to eat cod, the only food available, as the Spaniards do. They get drunk daily in frills and are on the verge of insubordination. Wellington tries to raise his morale, but they claim that they signed a contract with the army for their pay and sustenance; and that they do not fight for their country, like the Spaniards. The real losers are the civilians; the capital San Sebastian is devastated, of its 600 houses, only about 40 are unscathed; 1,500 families are homeless. An estimate will assess the material damages at 102 million real; not to mention the insults and crimes they suffered before the allied soldiers. Wellington will try to exonerate himself of the crimes committed by British soldiers against the civilian population, and his subsequent insubordinations, in a dispatch addressed to General Girón on September 28, saying: "... that I have at my command the scum of the land among all the nations of the world, it takes an iron hand to control them, and all kinds of information to discover their crimes ..."

9 – Austria: the Treaty of Toplitz is signed, formalizing the **SEVENTH COALITION**, made up of Russia, Prussia, England, Austria, Sweden, Spain, Portugal and several German states. Spain: General Manso's troops seize an Italian battalion in San Sadurní. In the siege of Pamplona: the besieged make another exit to show their determination, wounding and capturing Carlos of Spain with other officers and soldiers, but before returning to take refuge in the castle the garrison suffers about 100 casualties; Cassan will carry out similar actions to try to escape, knowing that he will not receive aid from France.

10- United States: A twenty-eight-year-old commodore named Oliver Hazard Perry had requested the mission to expel the British from Lake Erie. His request had been granted, although he had no vessel to carry it out. He himself had had to build in a few months his fleet of ten ships, the main one of which was the Lawrence, whose flag contained the words "do not deliver the ship", the last words of Captain Lawrence. Perry had been patrolling the lake for a month in search of the British fleet, and he found it this day. In a bitter battle he achieved the surrender of the British fleet, which put the lake at the mercy of the United States. This was of great tactical importance, since they could now easily transport men and supplies.

12 – Spain: Ordal combat. General Suchet leaves from his headquarters in Molins del Rey, north of Catalonia, with 30,000 French soldiers, with the purpose of attacking the highlands near Ordal, where the allied vanguard camps in the area, a division and four battalions commanded of General Adam; about 4,000 English, Spanish, Italian and Swiss, with several pieces of light artillery, supported by a cavalry squadron. At midnight, about 10,000 French from the division of Harispe, Delort, and Habert attack the Allied camp, wounding General Adam. The English withdraw after suffering many losses, leaving the Spaniards of the regiments of Aragon, Cadiz and Italians of several companies of Grenadiers of Ultonia, about 3,000 men. The attackers are rejected twice by the strong resistance of the defenders, until they flank the allies wrapping them in their rear, and force them to retreat to Villafranca and San Sadurní after an hour of intense fighting, which left 115 dead and 330 wounded.

13- Mexico: the Junta de Zitácuaro had dissolved, so José Maria Morelos convened the Congress of Chilpancingo, which this morning brought together ten deputies from as many Mexican provinces, including Ignacio Lopez Rayon.

14 – Spain: second combat of Villafranca.

15- Spain: decree of assimilation of the Indians, promulgated by the Cortes of Cadiz, by which all the missions with more than 100 years of antiquity are secularized, allowing the Indians to integrate into society and putting their lands in readiness to be purchased.

16- South America: not knowing that the Venezuelan port of La Guairá was in insurgent hands, arrives a convoy of 6 merchants with 1,200 soldiers and artillery stores, escorted by the frigate "Venganza" under the command of Captain Diego Prieto Gonzalez, upon entering The port is bombarded for an hour by the batteries, but they manage to escape, reaching Puerto Cabello afterwards.

18- South America: in Venezuela the Asturian José Tomas Boves, leading Spanish troops, enters Santa Ana, sacking the city and massacring its population, shortly after defeating Colonel Tomas Montilla in the battle of Santa Catalina.

21 – Spain: brief offensive by Moncada in Coll.

23- South America: at the request of the government of Chile, the "Argentine Auxiliary Battalion" leaves Mendoza, under the command of Marcos Gonzalez Balcarce and Juan Gregorio de Las Heras; crosses the Andes, are the first troops to act outside the viceroyalty, and enter this afternoon in Santiago.

25- South America: combat of Ancacato, in Bolivia, the royalist colonel Juan Saturnine Castro Gonzalez defeats and kills the republican caudillo Balthazar Cárdenas, who was in charge of 2,400 indigenous people of the Oruro region.

27- United States: willing to take advantage of Perry's victory, General Harrison crossed Lake Erie with 4,500 men and Procter had to retreat from Detroit. Tecumseh had opposed the withdrawal, but he could not afford to lose the protection of the One Arm Father (Procter was unmanly), and had to accompany him. The retreat was hasty with Harrison on their heels, until this afternoon they stopped by the River Thames in Canada, where Tecumseh managed to convince Procter of the need to present battle.

30- South America: Montverde Sunday receives reinforcements from Spain and counterattacks the Venezuelan separatists in front of an army of 3,000 men, but is defeated in Barbula by the troops of Atanasio Girardot, who died of a gunshot at the end of the battle, when he was about to plant the Venezuelan flag as a sign of his victory. That same day the Junta of Asunción appointed a government formed by two consuls who will alternately govern four months each. Lieutenant Colonel Fulgencio Yegros and Gaspar Rodriguez de Francia were elected consuls. In addition, a Congress or Paraguayan legislative chamber was formed.

Next book of this collection:
THE BATTLE OF LEIPZIG
The Campaign of France and the first abdication
1813-1814